NORTH CAROLINA'S
HISTORIC
RESTAURANTS

and their recipes

NORTH
CAROLINA'S

JOHN F. BLAIR, *Publisher*
Winston-Salem, North Carolina

HISTORIC
RESTAURANTS
and their recipes

by DAWN O'BRIEN

Drawings by Janice Murphy

Book design by Virginia Ingram
Drawings by Janice Murphy
Cover photographs by Bernard Carpenter
Composition by Graphic Composition, Inc.
Manufactured by Donnelley Printing Company

Library of Congress Cataloging in Publication Data on
page 206.

ACKNOWLEDGMENTS **W**ords seem insufficient to describe my thanks to the chefs who whispered, "This is the secret," as they showed me how they prepare a prized recipe, and to the owners who shared their restaurants' histories with me.

Multiple thanks to my editor, Audrey Kirby, who kept my participles from dangling.

I also thank the artist, Janice Murphy, for her pen and ink renderings of the restaurants.

A very special thank-you goes to Marty Rawson, Artie Rockwell, and Bev Wachtel for helping me test, retest, and correct many recipes.

A salute to the guinea pigs who downed as many as eight recipes in one sitting: Linda High; Tommy Peters; Frank and Lee Kecseti; Betty Jo Gilley; Jessica and Dick Roubaud; my husband, John; and my daughters, Daintry and Heather. And also to my cookie aficionado, Martin Sokoloff.

The award for courage, care, and criticism goes to the members of my writers' support group: John Brooks, Tom Collins, Diane and Justus Harris, Mark Moss, Irvin Prescott, Jim Roberts, and Nancy Young.

You can't say too much about encouragement, and I got a lot of it from my mother and my sisters and friends who are too many to name but who know who they are.

This book is dedicated to my daughters, Daintry and Heather. When Daintry discovered the nature of this project, she spontaneously uttered, "You know, Mother, the worst that could happen is you might learn how to cook!" And then there was my dear Heather, so often a victim of my culinary efforts, who swallowed and asked, "Does this mean more of your fancy do-dah meals?"

You see, prior to embarking upon this project, the only literary efforts my family connected me with were serious articles on health, the corporate climate, and public relations. My work was assigned, not chosen. It's a wonderful way to make a living, and for the most part I've enjoyed it. But when I began to notice my family's sly smiles when I attempted an ambitious recipe, I decided the time had come for me to exercise new options.

First, I approached my husband, and as the analytical person he is, he immediately wanted to know what I considered to be my credentials. I reminded him that I have a master's degree in communication from Wake Forest University, and that I have written dozens of training manuals and audiovisual programs for industry. He pointed out, however, that my education had not extended to the Cordon Bleu culinary institute.

Unsatisfied with his response, I decided to make a list. It read:
• I like to eat.
• I like to eat well.
• I like to eat well in beautiful old restaurants.
• I'd like to produce meals similar to those of gourmet chefs.
• I'd like to stay thin—well, reasonably.

This time, bypassing my usually supportive family, I went to my friend Jan with my problematic idea. Let me tell you about good friends. They know how to lie lovingly and will then tactfully help you solve the problem. For instance, when I admitted that I was no real cook, Jan effusively exclaimed,

"That's just not true. I've had excellent meals in your home."

"Yeah, but if it was good, it was probably one of my lucky accidents," I replied.

This is how she tactfully attacked my problem: "Look, you'll be going into the kitchen of every restaurant, where you can learn the tricks and secrets from the most experienced professional gourmet chefs in the state, right?"

"Right."

"You'll go home and test, modify, and adjust each recipe for family use, right?"

"Right."

"Well, there you are. If you can reproduce those recipes successfully, then anybody can."

See? Tact all the way.

The reason I chose historical restaurants is that I have a particular affinity for historical settings, and I want to see them preserved. Naturally, nothing pleased me more than to discover that the North Carolina Department of Cultural Resources has set up a section of its organization for the preservation of our structural heritage. This section helps coordinate programs for the rehabilitation of structures that have been designated as historically significant. As you might guess, the criteria for "historically significant" vary considerably. A basic consideration is age; the structure generally must be at least fifty years old. An equally important factor is the building's architectural integrity or uniqueness.

With the exception of two, all the restaurants in this book meet those requirements. The exceptions are the Angus Barn and the Villa Téo. Both restaurants were constructed from materials over a hundred years old, and by my criteria, that factor justifies identifying them as historically significant.

Remember how I said I wanted to do all this and stay thin? At the beginning, I didn't know if that was a realistic goal. I found that sometimes I could diet and enjoy myself as much as if I had ordered a heavier meal; other times I threw out the diet and explored the restaurant's more physically inflationary cuisine. How did I emerge? Well, I am still wearing the same dress size I wore fifty restaurants ago.

Comments from my family show that some things have changed, however. My younger daughter said, "Kirsten's mother wants to know if she can have that Coq au Vin recipe." My older daughter said, "Gee, Mama, the kids at school want me to show them how you make puff pastry look like a real fish."

"The Pecan Chicken is the best yet!" my husband told me.

"That's what you said last week about the Veal Oscar," I replied.

"I know, but you just keep topping yourself."

CONTENTS

STATE OF NORTH CAROLINA

OFFICE OF THE GOVERNOR

RALEIGH 27611

JAMES B. HUNT, JR.
GOVERNOR

     We are so proud of the great places in North Carolina which
give this state its great variety and essence. Even more important are
the hospitable people which give North Carolina its priceless reputation
as a friendly place.

     Our many historic restaurants add another dimension to the lore
of North Carolina and its special appeal. In this book, Dawn O'Brien has
captured a refreshing perspective of the state's culinary charms.

     The variety of 50 restaurants described here is as vast and
diverse as that of the state itself. They begin at the eastern shore,
near where the first Englishmen arrived four centuries ago. They extend
through the beautiful, urban Piedmont where much of what is good from the
past is still preserved. And they continue on to the mile high mountains
of Western North Carolina where breathtaking meals are matched by breathtaking views.

     This book is a special treasure of a very special part of
North Carolina.

Governor James B. Hunt, Jr.

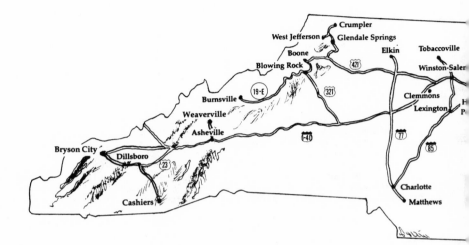

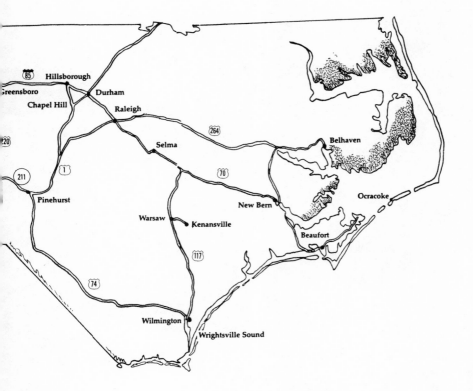

THE RIVER FOREST MANOR
Belhaven

THE RIVER FOREST MANOR

As you pass through the Ionic columns into the grandiose entrance hall of The River Forest Manor, try to picture a turn-of-the-century belle who lifts her voluminous skirt and ascends the elaborate stairway to the third-floor ballroom. Such a belle would have been the bride of railroad magnate John Aaron Wilkinson, who spared no expense or imagination to build this majestic mansion for his lady. Wilkinson employed Italian artists who had decorated Biltmore House at Asheville to adorn his ceilings with frescoes and to render the sun's rays in a three-dimensional effect through cleverly positioned beveled glass. The decor is itself a rich dessert that attracted then, as it does today, those who appreciate life's more refined offerings.

The culinary offerings of The River Forest Manor are even more copious now than when the mansion was turned into a restaurant by Axson Smith, Sr., in 1947. Axson, Jr., and his mother, Melba Smith, have continued to expand the epicurean repertoire of the famous smorgasbord, which attracts yacht owners who traverse the Intracoastal Waterway to moor their crafts virtually in the Manor's back yard.

The late Mr. Smith used to love telling of the time he looked out his back door and saw a man washing out his underwear on the deck of his yacht. A closer look revealed the launderer to be none other than Jimmy Cagney. Of course not all guests are that famous, but most yacht owners who wend their way up the Pungo River go there for no better reason than Mrs. Smith's oyster fritters, crabmeat casserole, and buttermilk hushpuppies. If those dishes fail to interest you, there are seventy-two delicious alternatives, plus a large selection of wine and beer.

You don't have to own a yacht in order to visit the Manor. Many of the landlubbers who overnight there enjoy the luxury of sleeping in a two-hundred-year-old bed and bathing in a tub built for two! One person sits at each end of the tub. And we thought the Victorian era was dull.

Speaking of bathing, dieters can melt away the smorgasbord in a hot tub outside, or they can carefully choose to dine on fresh vegetables, fruit salads, and broiled seafood. But since that would mean saying no to strawberry shortcake, you may feel inclined to follow the Manor's motto, "Eat, drink and be merry for tomorrow you may diet."

The River Forest Manor is located at 600 East Main Street in Belhaven. Dinner is served from 5:00 to 9:00 p. m. Monday through Saturday; Sundays from noon to 3:00 p. m. and from 5:00 p. m. to 9:00 p. m. For reservations call (919) 943-2151.

THE RIVER FOREST MANOR'S
MATTIE'S CARAMEL CAKE

2 sticks butter
2 cups sugar
4 large eggs

3 scant cups cake flour
3 scant teaspoons
   baking powder
1 cup lukewarm water

Cream butter and sugar. Beat eggs lightly and add to butter and sugar. Sift flour and baking powder together and add to mixture. Add water and beat well. Bake in three greased and floured 9-inch pans at 350 degrees until brown and springy, 25 to 30 minutes.

Cool and ice with caramel frosting (see recipe below).

THE RIVER FOREST MANOR'S
CARAMEL FROSTING

4 cups light brown sugar
1 cup evaporated milk
¼ teaspoon double-acting
   baking powder

3 tablespoons butter
2 cups chopped nut meats

Boil sugar, milk, and baking powder together until mixture comes to a soft boil (238 degrees). Remove from heat and stir in butter. Cool. Add nut meats and beat by hand until mixture is thick enough to spread.

THE RIVER FOREST MANOR'S
PEPPER STEAK

2 pounds sirloin steak
3 large green peppers
2 medium onions
1 cup water chestnuts
3 tablespoons oil
3 tablespoons soy sauce

2 tablespoons brown sugar
2 tablespoons cornstarch
1 teaspoon monosodium
  glutamate
½ cup white wine
½ cup water

3 fresh tomatoes

Cut steak in thin strips across the grain. Chop peppers, onions, and water chestnuts. Brown steak quickly in oil and remove from pan. Sauté peppers, onions, and water chestnuts. In a separate bowl, mix the soy sauce, brown sugar, cornstarch, monosodium glutamate, wine, and water. Combine sauce with the steak and vegetables, and cook 3 or 4 minutes.

Serve over hot saffron rice. Garnish with tomato wedges. Serves 4.

THE RIVER FOREST MANOR'S
PAMLICO CRABMEAT CASSEROLE

1 pound fresh crabmeat
1 cup chopped celery
½ cup chopped onions
1 cup mayonnaise
juice of 1 lemon

2 cups seasoned croutons
dash of red hot sauce
salt and pepper
½ cup fine bread crumbs
½ cup Parmesan cheese

½ stick butter

Combine everything but bread crumbs, butter, and cheese; place in a 2-quart casserole dish. Sprinkle with mixture of remaining ingredients. Bake at 350 degrees until casserole bubbles and has browned, 50 to 60 minutes. Serves 10 to 12.

ISLAND INN
Ocracoke

ISLAND INN

The ship, the *Ariosto*, was wrecked on a day when Mrs. Williams' kitchen on Ocracoke held "just a bit of shrimp and a bit of chicken," so she combined them. Her great-grandson, Larry, has embellished this recipe, making it one of the enticements of the Island Inn, but he gives credit for its origin to the inventive woman who needed to feed the survivors of that nineteenth-century disaster.

The resourcefulness of Ocracoke's residents is also evident from the many uses the inn has been given since it was built in 1901. The downstairs was used as a public school until the 1930's, and the crow's nest was officers' quarters during World War II. It was during the navy's stay that the island was so heavily sprayed with insecticides that frogs became extinct. Frogs were imported after the war, and they are now thriving, but their brief absence provoked Larry Williams' extensive frog collection in the Island Inn's lobby. You'll find many delicacies on the inn's menu, but Williams assures me that frog legs will never be one of them.

I especially enjoyed the appetizer of oysters with dill, and when I breakfast at the inn again, I'll have the oyster omelet. The Chicken and Shrimp Ariosto is a specialty that must be ordered in advance, but if you don't remember to call ahead, a recommendation is Edna's Crabcakes, which are especially good with a glass of wine or a beer. If you are looking for something a little lighter, investigate the selections listed on the menu as "for the light appetite."

Most visitors to Ocracoke would consider themselves out of luck to be on the island on a cold, rainy day, but that is when the inn is most likely to produce a pot of steaming black-eyed peas and onions. A day such as that would blend in well with the mood of the new decor of the dining room. It is helping the inn regain the look it had when it was first built.

The Island Inn is located on N. C. 12 in Ocracoke. Meals

are served from 7:00 a.m. to 9:30 p.m., seven days a week throughout the year. For reservations call (919) 928–4351.

ISLAND INN'S
SHE-CRAB SOUP WITH MARIGOLD

1 cup crabmeat,
  drained and flaked
2 cans cream of celery soup
3 cups milk
1 cup half-and-half
½ cup butter or margarine
2 boiled eggs, chopped

½ teaspoon Old Bay
  Seasoning
½ teaspoon Worcester-
  shire sauce
¼ teaspoon garlic salt
¼ teaspoon white pepper
¼ cup dry sherry

chopped marigold leaves

Combine soup, milk, cream, eggs, butter, Old Bay, Worcestershire, garlic, and pepper in a large Dutch oven; bring to a boil. Add crabmeat; cook over medium heat, stirring occasionally until heated through. Stir in sherry.

Sprinkle each serving with marigold leaves. Yields about 2 quarts.

ISLAND INN'S CHICKEN ELAINE

1 3- to 4-pound chicken
salt and pepper
3 tablespoons ketchup
3 tablespoons brown sugar
2 tablespoons Worcester-
  shire sauce
2 tablespoons melted butter

2 tablespoons vinegar
1 tablespoon lemon juice
1 small onion, chopped
1 clove garlic, pressed
1 teaspoon salt
1 teaspoon chili powder
1 teaspoon mustard

½ teaspoon cayene

Cut up chicken and season with salt and pepper. Lightly grease inside of brown paper bag; place chicken in bag. Combine remaining ingredients and pour over chicken. Roll up paper bag tightly at both ends. Place in a covered roasting pan. Bake at 350 degrees for 1 hour and 45 minutes. Serves 4.

ISLAND INN'S
SHRIMP AND CHICKEN ARIOSTO

1 3-pound broiler-fryer
1 pound fresh shrimp,
  peeled and deveined
1 stick butter or margarine
½ head cabbage, shredded
1 onion, sliced and
  separated into rings
2 10-ounce cans cream of
  chicken soup, undiluted
1 2-ounce jar diced
  pimiento, undrained

1 teaspoon soy sauce
¼ teaspoon granulated
  garlic
2 drops liquid smoke
salt and pepper
¼ cup dry white wine
lettuce leaves or
  cooked brown rice
chopped tomatoes
½ cup chopped
  salted peanuts

Boil chicken until tender; remove from bone and flake with a fork. Melt butter in a large Dutch oven; add chicken, shrimp, cabbage, and onion. Cook over medium heat until onion is tender. Stir soup, pimiento, soy sauce, garlic, and liquid smoke into meat mixture. Season to taste with salt and pepper. Simmer 15 minutes. Stir in wine, and cook 2 additional minutes over low heat.

Remove and serve on a lettuce-lined platter or over rice. Garnish with tomatoes and salted peanuts. Serves 6 to 8.

ISLAND INN'S KISS

½ ounce Galliano
colored sugar crystals

1 scoop vanilla ice cream

In a champagne glass, place ¼ ounce Galliano. Add ice cream. Pour another ¼ ounce Galliano over ice cream. Sprinkle with colored sugar crystals. Keep at room temperature until ice cream begins to melt. Place in freezer until ready to serve. Serves 1.

THE PELICAN RESTAURANT
Ocracoke

THE PELICAN RESTAURANT

The Pelican Restaurant might easily have been named Aunt Fanny's, after Fanny Howard. She and her husband, Billy, built this cottage in the 1880's. Since Fanny was known as one of Ocracoke's great cooks, it is most appropriate that her home now serves as one of the finest restaurants on the Outer Banks.

Back when Ocracoke was accessible only by boat, the cost of importing supplies to the island was high. That fact made the inhabitants a resourceful people who shared and took care of each other. Thus, when Billy Howard died in the early part of the century, the islanders built him a coffin. When it was completed, however, they discovered that the coffin was too short for its purpose. Unperturbed, Fanny waved the astounded workers aside, climbed into the coffin, and declared that it fit her perfectly. Another coffin was built for her husband, and the practical Fanny kept the first one in her bedroom for seventeen years. Neighbors claim that it became Fanny's favorite leisure-time retreat as well as her final resting place.

When renovating the cottage, Debbie and John Wells found an attic full of memorabilia, including a stack of early *Vogue* magazines. Can't you just envision Aunt Fanny getting comfy in her coffin with the latest *Vogue*?

I do believe that Fanny would most heartily approve of the large latticework front porch that so carefully has been added to the house. Although I dined in the evening, breakfast on the porch, which is sheltered by weeping willows and hundred-year-old live oaks, must be a very special way to begin the day.

For lunch, burgers and fresh fried fish net high marks. If you prefer something lighter, the curried chicken salad or marinated shrimp will help keep you looking fit in your bikini. But dinner is a different story. You could survive wonderfully on the marinated steak, but you've really blown it if you don't try the shrimp in caper butter or Coquilles St. Jacques. The more excellent is a matter of opinion. In addition, the catch of the day, which is prepared with one of the Pelican's special sauces, is bound to be an improvement over the catch from your local supermarket. The Pelican also provides a small but good choice of wines.

The desserts are outrageous, especially the chocolate brandy cheesecake. Even a sliver will kiss your calorie counter goodbye. There are, however, times and places at which the wisdom of dieting and the wisdom of gourmet dining meet in conflict. The Pelican Restaurant is one of those delightful places.

The Pelican Restaurant is located on N. C. 12 across from the post office in Ocracoke. Breakfast is served from 7:00 to 11:00 a. m., lunch from 11:00 a. m. to 2:30 p. m., and dinner from 5:00 to 9:00 p. m., seven days a week from May 1 to October 15. For reservations call (919) 928–6611.

THE PELICAN RESTAURANT'S
MARINATED VEGETABLES

Vegetables:
12 green beans, left long
2 medium zucchini, sliced

**2 stalks broccoli, cut up
and stems removed**

Dressing:
⅔ cup salad oil
½ cup chopped pimiento
⅓ cup red wine vinegar
1 tablespoon capers
**1 tablespoon Grey Poupon
mustard**

½ cup chopped scallions
**¼ teaspoon each of:
rosemary, thyme,
granulated garlic,
paprika, dry mustard,
honey, salt, and cayenne**

Steam vegetables separately until crunchy and bright green. Cool.

For dressing, stir all ingredients together until well blended. Pour over vegetables. Toss and chill 1 hour or longer. Serves 4 to 6.

THE PELICAN RESTAURANT'S
SHRIMP IN CAPER BUTTER

40 raw, fresh shrimp,
  peeled and deveined
3½ cups cooked long-grain
  white rice
1 stick butter
½ cup diced pimientoes
½ cup capers
½ cup diced scallions

1 teaspoon granulated garlic
1 teaspoon whole thyme
¼ cup dry vermouth
¾ cup chicken stock
4 cherry tomatoes
2 tablespoons chopped
  fresh parsley

Foam butter in large skillet. When bubbles dissipate, add shrimp, pimientoes, capers, scallions, garlic, and thyme. Cover and cook on high heat until shrimp turn pink. Add vermouth, then chicken stock; cook one minute. Add parsley, rice, and tomatoes. Stir well; cover for one minute or until heated through. Serves 4.

THE PELICAN RESTAURANT'S
ZUCCHINI, SOUR CREAM, AND DILL

4 medium zucchini

3 tablespoons butter

Sauce:
3 tablespoons sour cream
2 tablespoons Parmesan
  cheese

1 tablespoon dill weed
½ teaspoon salt
dash of granulated garlic

Slice zucchini. Sauté in butter until bright green. Remove and place in a bowl.

Combine ingredients for sauce and pour over sautéed zucchini. Serve at once. Serves 4 to 6.

CLAWSON'S EMPORIUM
Beaufort

CLAWSON'S EMPORIUM

Clawson's Emporium has been in business in the same place since 1905; the delectable difference is that it has been transformed from a grocery and bakery into a restaurant with two saloons. Bill Rogers bought the building in 1977 and began to uncover what the years had hidden—tin ceiling, pine flooring, and old brick walls. A brick courtyard behind the restaurant is where Mr. Clawson did his baking. When he was annoyed by flies, he simply whipped out his gun and shot them off the wall. Retaining that spirit, The Bakery is now a frontier-style saloon, with overtones of an English pub. From what I can see and hear, only the musical entertainment has been updated; it includes bluegrass and rock.

After circling back into the unpretentious atmosphere of the restaurant, I ordered the dish that has made Clawson's famous. It is appropriately named The Original Dirigible: It wouldn't take many to transform your appearance into that of a blimp. The Dirigible is a huge baked potato stuffed with cheeses, seafood, sour cream, and other tasties that respond well to a glass of chablis or your favorite beer. For your benefit (which turned out also to be mine), I sampled the clam chowder. I was unsuccessful at wheedling that recipe for you, but I did succeed in getting the strawberry crepe, which adds a nice dessert touch to any meal.

At dinner you can still have the Dirigible, but baby barbecued ribs, steaks, and fresh seafood always claim center stage. If you prefer a lighter meal in the summer, you can dip into the salad bar, which is cleverly set up in one of those old tin Coca-Cola coolers that some of us used to squander a whole nickel on. During the winter, Clawson's offers dieters a list of choices from a local diet center's recipes. In the summer— well, Rogers philosophizes that summer is vacation time, and that means a vacation from diets as well. After all, you've got the whole winter to repair the damage. As I continued with another bite of the Dirigible, that philosophy began to grow on me.

Clawson's Emporium is located at 429 Front Street in Beaufort. Hours vary greatly according to the day and season. For reservations call (919) 728–2133.

CLAWSON'S EMPORIUM'S
DEVILED CRAB

½ pound crabmeat
(claw meat, if possible)
3 tablespoons butter
½ cup chopped green
  pepper
1 cup chopped onion
¼ cup flour
½ 6-ounce can
  evaporated milk

1 tablespoon yellow
  mustard
1 tablespoon Worcester-
  shire sauce
1 tablespoon Lawry's sauce
1 teaspoon Texas Pete
1 cup chopped hard-boiled
  eggs, about 3
1½ cups bread crumbs

6 to 8 crab shells or ramekins

Melt butter and sauté peppers and onions until transparent. Add crabmeat and cook about 2 minutes. Remove from heat. In a separate bowl, mix flour and enough evaporated milk to form a pourable paste. Add crabmeat mixture, mixing thoroughly. Season with mustard, Worcestershire, Lawry's sauce, and Texas Pete. Blend remainder of evaporated milk, bread crumbs and eggs into mixture. Spoon even amounts into lightly greased shells. Bake at 350 degrees for 20 minutes or until golden brown. Serves 6 to 8.

CLAWSON'S EMPORIUM'S
ORIGINAL DIRIGIBLE

1 1-pound potato
1 tablespoon butter
1 tablespoon chopped
  onion
1 tablespoon chopped
  green pepper
⅛ cup diced ham
⅛ cup diced turkey

⅛ cup shredded
  Provolone cheese
⅛ cup shredded
  cheddar cheese
¼ cup sour cream
pinch of chives
2 slices cooked bacon,
  crumbled

Bake potato at 400 degrees for 1 hour or until done. Split open and rake with fork. Work in butter, onion, and pepper; work in diced ham, turkey, and cheeses. Close potato and heat until cheese melts. Remove and top with sour cream, chives, and bacon.

For a seafood Dirigible, substitute cooked, minced crab and shrimp for ham and turkey. Serves 1.

CLAWSON'S EMPORIUM'S
STRAWBERRY CREPE

8 crepes (see Index)
½ cup sour cream
1 cup cream cheese,
  softened

4 teaspoons brown sugar
2 cups sliced
  fresh strawberries

Combine sour cream and cream cheese. Spread 2 table-spoons of mixture on each crepe. Top with about ¼ cup strawberries and sprinkle with brown sugar to taste. Fold crepe and place seam-side-down in a baking dish. Heat until warmed through. Serves 8.

HARVEY MANSION
New Bern

HARVEY MANSION

When you arrive at Harvey Mansion, which is commandingly positioned on the Trent River, turn your memory back to 1791. Think of old John Harvey directing shipments of cargo from the warehouse inside his home onto the merchant ships anchored below. History reports that this wealthy plantation owner from Shropshire, England, owned thirty slaves. It was, no doubt, the slaves who hauled those bales of barley and tobacco from the plantation across town to the store and warehouse, and from there onto the ships.

Today, as you enter the Mansion, you are still greeted by the hand-carved rosewood staircase that has been authentically restored through the generosity of Robert and Cora Clark. Each of the six dining rooms has been wallpapered and decorated in the Federal style to preserve the atmosphere of the era in which the house was built. The Mansion's original kitchen, which now serves as the cocktail lounge, is a cozier setting, with its exposed brick and its handsome brass and teak bar. The warehouse also has been refitted to accommodate a stage, where guests are entertained with Broadway musicals in a cabaret setting.

The Mansion's owner, Dave Thurston, tells me that he feels the restaurant, bar, and theater fit in well with the vigorous spirit of John Harvey, who died at the age of seventy-four, shortly after the birth of a daughter. So, each October 10, the Mansion throws a birthday party to celebrate and honor its originator. Last year the staff prepared a special Baked Alaska for eighty.

You didn't think I forgot about the food, did you? *Southern Living* magazine described the Mansion's continental menu as having "touches of the lighter nouvelle cuisine."

My favorite entrée is the Veal Grecian, which is veal that has been panned in butter and is served with a special sauce of cheeses on a bed of eggplant. If you prefer to diet through lunch or dinner, then Thurston suggests you feast on the local fresh seafood that is broiled in herbs and wine. If not dieting, try the Tryon Palace Scampi. It is a wonderful concoction of large fan-tailed shrimp stuffed with crabmeat, wrapped in bacon, and then broiled.

Harvey Mansion is located at 221 Tryon Palace Drive in New Bern. Lunch is served from 11:00 a. m. to 2:00 p. m., and dinner from 6:00 to 10:00 p. m., Tuesday through Sunday. The lounge opens at 4:00 p. m. For reservations call (919) 638–3205.

HARVEY MANSION'S COUNTRY CAPTAIN

5 chicken breasts
4 green peppers
2 large yellow onions
1 stick unsalted butter
  or margarine
½ tablespoon curry powder
½ cup or more canned
  tomatoes, crushed
¼ cup strong beef stock
  (see recipe below)

¼ cup strong chicken stock
  (see recipe below)
1 bay leaf
salt and pepper
flour
oil for frying
3 to 4 tablespoons toasted
  almonds
3 to 4 tablespoons raisins

Remove the seeds and membrane from the peppers and cut into ½-inch squares. Dice the onions. In a large skillet, sauté the onions and peppers until transparent. Add curry and stir until well mixed with butter. If the vegetables begin to stick, add 3 more tablespoons butter. Add the tomatoes and stir over high heat. Add the beef stock, chicken stock, and bay leaf. Simmer uncovered on low heat, stirring occasionally, for 90 minutes.

Lightly salt and pepper the chicken breasts and dredge them in the flour. Shake off excess flour and fry chicken in oil until golden brown.

Place the cooked chicken in a casserole dish. Pour the sauce over the chicken and cover. Bake at 350 degrees for 45 minutes.

Sprinkle with toasted almonds and raisins before serving. Serves 3 to 5.

HARVEY MANSION'S
CHICKEN OR BEEF STOCK

3 to 4 pounds chicken or
  beef bones
2 carrots

2 stalks celery
1 to 2 onions
2 tablespoons butter

½ cup red wine or vermouth

Brown bones in oven at 375 degrees for ½ hour. Chop carrots, celery, and onions; sauté in butter. Pour vegetables and liquid into a large pot; add bones and water to cover. Add wine or vermouth and simmer for 4 hours until mixture is reduced. Strain off fat and store in covered containers in freezer for later use.

The yield depends on how much the stock has been reduced.

HARVEY MANSION'S BÉARNAISE SAUCE

4 tablespoons white wine
4 tablespoons white vinegar
4 teaspoons minced shallots

2 teaspoons dried tarragon
6 egg yolks
2 sticks butter

white pepper

In a saucepan, cook white wine, vinegar, shallots, and tarragon until the mixture is reduced by ⅓. Place it in a food processor with the steel blade, and process with the egg yolks, switching on and off. Heat the butter to boiling; add butter to mixture in processor, pouring it through the tube in a steady stream. Season with pepper to taste.

For range method, use a double boiler to combine the eggs with wine, shallots, vinegar, and tarragon. Stir constantly until blended; slowly add the melted butter. Makes 1½ cups.

HENDERSON HOUSE
New Bern

HENDERSON HOUSE

Usually a restaurant excels in either cuisine, atmosphere, decor, or history, but at Henderson House each category rivals the other. The house is a three-story brick structure believed to have been built in 1799 for Thomas Haslen, a member of Governor William Tryon's Royal Council. Later, when Haslen escaped to the Bahamas, he deeded the house to his daughter in gratitude for "love and affection."

During the Civil War, the house was requisitioned for quarters by Company D of the 45th Massachusetts Volunteer Militia. After that episode it settled down to normal, if you can call housing two friendly ghosts "normal." On the third floor is a shop that carries rag dolls and toys made by the restaurant's owner, Alice Fay Grant. At first, the Grants sought all kinds of reasons to explain why the dolls and toys stored on shelves at closing time were found on the floor on more than one morning, as if a child had been playing with them. Only after researching the history of the house did the Grants discover that a nine-year-old boy died there, and that his mother died some years later. She is a very peaceful spirit, but apparently the little boy can't resist a child's temptations from time to time.

During the Grants' restoration of the house, they found trapdoors and secret places where it is possible that either valuables or people were once hidden in times of danger. The dining rooms, with Federal mantels and handmade moldings, have been decorated in "Tryon Palace ballroom blue," which has a decidedly green cast. The fourteen-foot ceilings are covered in a light moire silk, and the room contains its original floor-to-ceiling gold leaf mirror. The Federal-style decor has been carried even to the dust-capped waitresses with their long calico aprons.

The day I lunched at Henderson House was a bit nippy, so I ordered a pot of tea. With splendid attention to detail, my teapot was kept hot with an English tea cozy. The Epicurean Sandwich is a meal in itself, with ham and turkey baked under a delicate mushroom sauce. I also sampled the chicken salad, which was the best I've ever tasted. It had large chunks of chicken in a light sauce that hinted of herbs. Another little marvel is broiled crabmeat and cheese, which is laced with spices and served on an English muffin. The homemade muffins are another treat, especially when accented with honey butter. For dessert I had a scrumptious meringue shell topped with ice cream, chocolate sauce, and brandied fruit. If dieting I would have opted for the chicken salad with a fruit cup or Mrs. Grant's famous cold peach soup.

For the evening fare I would choose the Seafood Supreme, which is shrimp, crabmeat, and mushrooms baked in a cheese and sherry sauce. The wine list ranges from an inexpensive wine cooler to Piper Hiedsieck champagne.

Even the most finicky connoisseur would be hard-pressed to register a complaint against this restaurant, which tries to make every customer as comfortable as possible. Once, the management even arranged a small table in a private room for a woman who insisted upon dining with her dog.

In case you're wondering, the restaurant is named after its previous owner. "After all," explained Mrs. Grant, "the only possible worse name in the South than Sherman is Grant."

Henderson House is located at 216 Pollock Street in New Bern. Lunch is served from 11:00 a. m. to 2:00 p. m. Tuesday through Saturday, and dinner from 6:30 to 8:30 p. m. Friday and Saturday. For reservations call (919) 637–4784.

HENDERSON HOUSE'S COLD PEACH SOUP

3 cups peaches and juice   **1 cup sour cream or yogurt**
  (fresh, frozen, or canned)   **½ teaspoon almond extract**

Place skinned and chopped peaches with other ingredients into a blender and blend until frothy.

Serve chilled. Will keep a day or so. Serves 4.

Excellent for sufferers of flu or sore throat, or on a hot day.

HENDERSON HOUSE'S MUFFINS

2 eggs
3 tablespoons melted butter
¾ cup milk
1 teaspoon or more vanilla
2 cups self-rising flour

½ teaspoon salt
½ cup sugar
paper muffin liners
  (optional)
Pam spray

Before preheating oven to 425 degrees, adjust one rack to upper third of oven and other rack to lower third of oven.

Mix all liquid ingredients in the blender. Combine dry ingredients in a bowl; add liquid mixture and stir with a wooden spoon until quite smooth. Put paper liners in muffin tins and spray with Pam. Fill ½ to ⅔ full and bake at 425 degrees until golden on top, about 20 to 25 minutes. Be sure to rotate the muffins from the bottom to the top shelf halfway through baking. Yields 24.

HENDERSON HOUSE'S HONEY BUTTER

1¼ stick butter, softened   ¼ cup honey
¾ cup confectioner's sugar

Mix ingredients until smooth and spreadable.

Honey butter can be stored for a long time in a covered jar in the refrigerator. Yields 2 cups.

POPLAR GROVE PLANTATION
Wilmington

POPLAR GROVE
PLANTATION

Poplar Grove Plantation was on the list of restaurants in historical settings that was given to me by the North Carolina Department of Cultural Resources, so why no one knew where it was located remains a mystery to this day.

Having finished the restaurants in Wilmington, I was on my way out of town, took a wrong turn and "found" Poplar Grove Plantation. The caretaker, Mr. Norris, was just leaving when I arrived and explained my interest in the restaurant. He gallantly gave me a personally guided tour through one of the most beautifully restored plantation homes that I have ever visited. He left out no detail, not even the cypress balcony porches that slant to allow the rain to drain naturally.

Historians have recorded that this was the state's first peanut-producing plantation, purchased in 1795 by James Foy, Jr., the son of a Revolutionary War hero. It wasn't until 1850 that the present house, an immense two-story Greek Revival frame house, was built by Joseph M. Foy. He was the son of James Foy, Jr., and is renowned as a pioneering champion of human rights. I am told that examples of his progressive beliefs in equality are demonstrated today in the costumed "living dramas" that are held at the house. The dramas take place in the rooms where similar conversations are believed to have been held between Foy and his slaves. Grievances were heard, discussed, and acted upon accordingly, which was an unprecedented arrangement during that era.

It appears that other generations of the Foys were able to extend their philosophy of human rights to include women. This is evident from the fact that Aunt Nora, who married James T. Foy and came to the plantation in 1871, later became the postmistress. Aunt Nora died in 1923, and I am told that her spirit continues to be felt from time to time. It is said that at night she can be heard pacing upstairs in what was her bedroom. And on the night of the annual candlelight tour, a glow has been seen at Aunt Nora's window long after the guests departed and all the candles were extinguished.

I regret that I found the plantation too late to have tasted the restaurant's fare, which is prepared by recipes that have been handed down from family heads, old slave cooks, and mammies. I have tested the recipes that have been so generously shared with me, however. If the coconut pie, originated by Aunt Betty, mistress of the plantation at the turn of the century, is any indication of the present dining room's quality, my sweet tooth would give it a high mark. My whole family felt that the Chicken Fantastic is appropriately named. The manager of Poplar Grove Plantation, Nancy Simon, recommended the stuffed tomatoes or a plate of fruit and cottage cheese for dieters.

The dining room also serves Sunday dinners, which have waiting lines that extend up the driveway, another good indication of the food's quality. The Christmas menu also sounds very special. It features either ham, turkey, or roast pork, with pineapple sweet potatoes, pecan pie, cranberry Waldorf salad, and a glass of house wine, all for less money than I can prepare a Christmas meal myself. At any time of the year, you have the privilege of ordering wines that come from neighboring Duplin County.

The Plantation's azalea blossoms were at their peak when I visited, but I'd like to return at Christmas to see for myself the burning candle in Aunt Nora's window. I would like to try to initiate some kind of communication with her—but perhaps she has already communicated with me. After all, I, who am a seasoned traveler, did take the "wrong" road that led me directly to Poplar Grove Plantation. Isn't that curious?

Poplar Grove Plantation is located at Scott's Hill, nine miles north of Wilmington on U. S. 17. Lunch is served from 11:30 a. m. to 3:00 p. m. Monday through Saturday, and dinner is served from noon to 6:00 p. m. Sundays only. For reservations call (919) 686–9503.

POPLAR GROVE PLANTATION'S
CHICKEN FANTASTIC

1 3- or 4-pound chicken,
  cut up
½ stick butter
1 package frozen French-cut
  green beans, thawed
1 can cream of celery soup
1 can cream of mushroom
  soup

1 can water chestnuts,
  chopped
½ cup mayonnaise
3 tablespoons chopped
  onion
3 teaspoons chopped
  pimiento

Brown chicken in butter and place in greased casserole dish. Combine remaining ingredients and pour over chicken. Bake at 350 degrees for 40 minutes.

Serve over wild rice. Serves 8.

POPLAR GROVE'S PLANTATION CAKE

2 sticks butter, melted
2 cups sugar
⅔ cup milk
2 eggs, beaten

2 teaspoons vanilla
2 cups plain flour
2 teaspoons baking powder

Cream butter and sugar together; add milk, eggs, and vanilla. Combine flour and baking powder and add to other ingredients, mixing thoroughly. Pour into 13- by 9- by 2-inch greased and floured pan. Bake at 350 degrees for 30 to 35 minutes.

POPLAR GROVE PLANTATION'S
AUNT BETTY'S COCONUT PIE

¼ stick margarine, softened
1½ cups sugar
1½ cups evaporated milk
1½ cups flake coconut

3 eggs, beaten
1 tablespoon flour
  or cornstarch
1 teaspoon vanilla

1 9-inch pie shell, unbaked

Cream sugar and margarine. Mix remaining ingredients, pour into pie shell, and bake at 350 degrees for 30 minutes.

STEMMERMAN'S 1855
Wilmington

STEMMERMAN'S 1855 Inevitably, the City of Wilmington discovers another tunnel whenever it digs underground near the Cape Fear River. Each discovery adds to an intricate network of tunnels that once functioned as a conduit for the blockade runners during the Civil War.

Charles Stemmerman ran a seemingly innocent grocery store on Front Street, but his downstairs warehouse served a dangerous function. Even today as you pass the brick and ballast-stone walls at the last curve of the stairway, you can see where a large tunnel was sealed over. Moving my hand over the seal, I thought of the people who had crept through that tunnel to the harbor exit, and of the smuggled munitions that were stored in that warehouse.

I closed my eyes as I sat in a high wooden booth, and scenes of courage and heroism flickered through my mind. I wondered if the rather exorbitant $10,500 Stemmerman had paid for his grocery store operation in 1855 had been recouped by his trafficking in military supplies.

My dinner companion brought me back to reality when our wonderful appetizer of bacon and oysters, called Angels on Horseback, arrived. It was followed by the restaurant's famous and delicious Flounder Marguery and the Sour Cream Chicken, and was topped off by a fantastic dessert of Chocolate Truffle Cake. We were certainly not counting calories that night, as I had the day before at lunch, when I had the seafood salad on the upstairs veranda.

The veranda, with its tranquilizing view of the river, is adjacent to the original grocery area, which has been transformed into an attractive dining room with exposed brick and stained glass windows. The view from the veranda set me to wonder if the same boats transporting supplies to the Confederacy could have hidden runaway slaves. Stranger tales have been told. This is what I really appreciate about Stemmerman's—not only is it satisfying to your taste buds, but its rich history stimulates your imagination.

Stemmerman's 1855 is located at 138 South Front Street in Wilmington. Lunch is served Monday through Saturday from 11:30 a. m. to 3:00 p. m., and dinner from 5:00 to 10:00 p. m. For reservations call (919) 763-0248.

STEMMERMAN'S ANGELS ON HORSEBACK

12 slices bacon
12 oysters
12 toothpicks
chopped parsley

paprika
½ cup sour cream
2 tablespoons horseradish

Fry bacon until half done. Remove from skillet and lay out on a cookie sheet. Place one oyster on center of bacon and sprinkle with parsley and paprika. Roll bacon over oyster and secure with a toothpick. Bake at 350 degrees until bacon crisps. Meanwhile, mix sour cream and horseradish together. When bacon and oysters are done, spoon sauce over them. Serves 4.

STEMMERMAN'S FLOUNDER MARGUERY

8 ½-pound flounder fillets
¼ pound shrimp, split
   lengthwise
1 cup oysters with liquor
½ stick butter
⅓ cup flour
½ pound mushrooms,
   sliced
1 teaspoon butter

1¾ cups half and half
3 tablespoons lemon juice
5 tablespoons sherry
½ teaspoon paprika
¼ teaspoon salt
¼ teaspoon white pepper
more salt and pepper to
   taste

Melt butter in a saucepan; stir in flour, making a roux, until the flour takes on a nutty aroma. Do not brown. In a separate saucepan sauté the mushrooms in the teaspoon of butter. To the roux add the half and half, lemon juice, sherry, paprika, salt and pepper, shrimp, and oysters and liquor; heat to the boiling point, stirring with wire whisk to remove lumps. Add the mushrooms, and more salt and pepper to taste; simmer a few more minutes while the flavors combine.

As sauce simmers, broil flounder until flaky. Remove from broiler and cover with sauce. Serves 8.

STEMMERMAN'S SOUR CREAM CHICKEN

5 ½-pound chicken breasts
1 pint sour cream
½ cup lemon juice
1 ounce medium dry sherry
3 cloves garlic, minced

1 tablespoon celery salt
½ tablespoon salt
¼ teaspoon paprika
¼ teaspoon black pepper
1 cup bread crumbs

Combine sour cream, lemon juice, sherry, garlic, celery salt, salt, paprika, and pepper in bowl and mix thoroughly. Skin chicken breasts and place in marinade; refrigerate for at least 24 hours.

When ready to cook, spread chicken breasts flat on a greased sheet and sprinkle tops with bread crumbs to cover. Bake at 350 degrees for 10 to 12 minutes or until the meat is firm.

Place each breast in a bed of herbed long-grain and wild rice. Serves 5.

RIVERVIEW RESTAURANT
Wilmington

**RIVERVIEW
RESTAURANT**

Its location above the Cape Fear River is what led Mary Ann and Francois Fotre to name the 120-year-old home that houses their restaurant the Riverview. I have never been one to downplay the pleasure of a view, but this one, in my opinion, is upstaged by the decor of the house, which reminded me of Thomas Gray's phrase, "thoughts that breathe." Somehow the decorator has captured an eighteenth-century ambiance and has even given it breath. You feel this from the moment you give your name to Mrs. Fotre, who checks your reservation at a hand-carved oak icebox still bearing its brass-plated name, the North Pole.

The dining areas have retained their regal mahogany and tile fireplaces and the mantel mirrors that reflect the glow from the satin-glass and crystal light fixtures. I especially loved the rich royal-blue velvet chairs that contrast so smoothly with the peach-colored linen tablecloths, the flowers, and the drapery swags that give balance to fragile lace curtains. However, the room with the best view of the river is decorated in a more casual atmosphere. It has the feel of a porch, with ladder-back chairs, brown print tablecloths, and Tiffany lamps.

If the decorator has given breath to thought, then Fotre, the chef, does no less with the food. This should come as no surprise, since Fotre was awarded the Golden Pan award from Maxims in Paris before he went to New York and opened both Maxwell's Plum and Regine's.

When I asked him how he got to Wilmington, North Carolina, he smiled and said, "I was asked to open a restaurant in Wilmington, and I thought they meant Delaware."

This is one mistake of which I, along with a few thousand others, have become the rich beneficiary.

I selected a very dry white wine to accompany my appetizer of fresh oysters covered with spinach and Béarnaise sauce. I followed this with veal sweetbreads in Madeira sauce. If you are thinking in terms of a lighter meal, the fresh flounder poached in wine would be an excellent choice. For dessert I couldn't resist the Cherries Jubilee. What an encore to an evening of culinary mastery.

The Riverview Restaurant is located at 226 South Front Street in Wilmington. Dinner is served from 6:00 to 10:00 p. m. Monday through Saturday. For reservations call (919) 763–5767.

OYSTERS RIVERVIEW

12 large oysters
12 oyster shells
3 tablespoons unsalted
  butter
¼ cup flour
2 cups scalded milk
⅓ cup oyster liquid
4 scallions, chopped

¼ cup cooked spinach,
  chopped and drained
⅓ cup grated
  Parmesan cheese
dash of nutmeg
1 teaspoon salt
¼ teaspoon pepper
1 cup Béarnaise sauce
  (see Index)

Melt butter over moderate heat and add flour to make a roux; cook for about three minutes. Remove from heat and gradually add milk and half of oyster liquid; whisk until smooth. Bring sauce to a boil, reduce heat, then add scallions and simmer for 15 minutes. Add spinach, cheese, nutmeg, and salt and pepper. Put some of the oysters in each of the shells and moisten with remaining oyster liquid. Divide spinach sauce among shells, covering oysters completely. Top each with 1½ tablespoons Béarnaise sauce. Serves 2 to 3.

RIVERVIEW'S SHRIMP SCAMPI

10 jumbo shrimp, cooked
2 tablespoons butter
1 large tomato, chopped

1 teaspoon salt
¼ teaspoon pepper
1½ cups white wine

35

1 clove garlic, minced
heavy pinch of basil
heavy pinch of oregano

2 tablespoons chicken stock
(see Index)

Sauté garlic and tomatoes in butter. Add seasonings, chicken stock, and wine. Bring sauce to a boil, then lower heat and cook for two minutes. Pour sauce over shrimp in a shallow baking dish. Place 4 inches beneath the heat and broil for 4 to 6 minutes.

Serve over rice. Serves 2.

RIVERVIEW'S VEAL SWEETBREADS
IN MADEIRA SAUCE

6 ounces veal sweetbreads
flour for dredging
1 tablespoon oil
1 tablespoon butter
1 shallot, chopped
3 large fresh mushrooms,
  sliced

½ cup Madeira wine
¼ cup beef stock
  (see Index)
1 tablespoon heavy cream
¼ cup cognac or good
  brandy

Slice sweetbreads very thin. Lightly dredge in flour, then sauté in butter and oil. Remove veal, drain pan, and sauté the shallots and mushrooms. Add wine, beef stock, and cream. Heat through.

Pour sauce over sweetbreads, flambé with cognac, and serve at once. Serves 1.

THE GRAHAM HOUSE INN
Kenansville

THE GRAHAM HOUSE INN

As I approached the antebellum Graham House Inn, framed with live oaks draped in Spanish moss, I thought, "Ah, this is from my century, a time when architects used no shortcuts in building a home." I became an even stronger advocate once inside the Italianate mansion. The heart-pine floors, ten working fireplaces, and eight-foot windows attest to the craftsmanship that could be had when Dr. Chauncey Graham built this house in 1855.

Currently, each of the dining rooms carries through a metal motif, handsomely decorated in either copper, pewter, or brass. I was particularly impressed with the eighteenth-century wine cellar, complete with wines from the nearby Duplin Winery. While some of the wine ferments in kegs in the cellar, the majority comes from the winery already bottled. Now, this is where good old Southern ingenuity has one-upped the county liquor law: Before dinner you may make your selection at a wine-tasting bar in the stone-walled wine cellar; then you can buy a bottle to "brown bag" at your table. With strategy like that, it's odd that the South lost the war.

Two things certainly have not been lost. One is an Old-South attitude toward gracious dining, and the other is those famous Colonial recipes. The best reason for getting out of bed in the morning is The Graham House Inn's breakfast buffet. It offers twelve hearty items at a price so low that it boggles credibility. It would also bulge my belt, so I opted for dinner, which is served by waitresses in antebellum costumes. Desiring a light meal, I chose the Chicken Carolina, which is chicken cooked with vegetables and served on a bed of wild rice. If you want to keep even further from calories, co-owner Jean Stephens recommends salmagundi. This is a Colonial salad that helped retain those eighteen-inch waistlines. Unable to suppress my curiosity, I asked for a bite of a sweet potato muffin. Let me tell you, there's no such thing as one bite, which is why I begged for the recipe. Whatever your choice, you are certain to succumb to the inn's motto, "Come sup with us and enjoy."

The Graham House Inn is located at the corners of Cooper and Main streets in Kenansville. Breakfast is served from 6:30 a. m., lunch from 11:00 a. m., and dinner from 6:00 p. m., Tuesday through Saturday. Dinner is served from noon to 6:00 p. m. on Sunday. For reservations call (919) 296–1122.

THE GRAHAM HOUSE INN'S
SWEET POTATO MUFFINS

1¾ cups all-purpose flour
¼ cup sugar
1 tablespoon baking
 powder
1 tablespoon brown sugar
1 teaspoon salt
½ teaspoon cinnamon

pinch of nutmeg
1¼ cups mashed cooked
 sweet potatoes
¼ cup margarine, melted
2 eggs, slightly beaten
¼ cup sugar
¾ cup milk

Sift dry ingredients together. Combine sweet potatoes, margarine, eggs, sugar, and milk; stir well. Add dry ingredients, mixing just until moistened. Spoon into greased muffin tin, filling cups ⅔ full. Bake at 300 degrees for 45 minutes. Yields 18.

THE GRAHAM HOUSE INN'S
QUICHE LORRAINE

8 slices bacon,
 cooked and crumbled
2 ounces pepperoni,
 chopped
1½ cups shredded Swiss
 cheese

4 eggs, beaten
2 cups half-and-half
¾ teaspoon salt
⅛ teaspoon pepper
1 9-inch pie shell, unbaked

Combine bacon, pepperoni, eggs, cream, and salt and pepper with 1 cup cheese. Place in pie shell, and bake at 425 degrees for 15 minutes, then reduce to 300 degrees and bake 30 to 35 minutes longer. Top with remaining cheese. Serves 6.

THE GRAHAM HOUSE INN'S
CHICKEN CREPES

Filling:

2 cups chopped, cooked chicken

½ 10-ounce can cream of mushroom soup

⅓ cup shredded Muenster cheese

2 tablespoons chopped onions

2 tablespoons fresh parsley

salt and pepper

Crepes:

1 cup flour

1 teaspoon salt

1 cup milk

3 eggs

2 tablespoons vegetable oil

dash of paprika

Sauce:

½ can cream of mushroom soup

⅓ cup shredded Muenster cheese

1 tablespoon chopped fresh parsley

½ cup milk

Combine ingredients for filling and set aside for later use. Combine ingredients for sauce and heat until cheese is melted.

For crepes, combine flour and salt. Put milk, eggs, oil, and dry ingredients in blender, and blend until smooth. Refrigerate for 1 hour.

Brush bottom of crepe pan with oil and heat until hot but not smoking. Place 3 tablespoons of batter in pan and cook about 1 minute; flip and cook about 30 seconds. Cook all crepes, keeping them warm while separated with waxed paper.

Spoon ⅓ cup chicken onto each crepe and roll it up. Place crepes seam-down in baking pan and pour sauce over them. Cook at 350 degrees for about 20 minutes. Sprinkle with paprika and serve immediately. Serves 5 to 6.

THE COUNTRY SQUIRE
Warsaw

THE COUNTRY SQUIRE

The moment I stepped out of the rain and into the dim torch-lit, brick-floored hearth room at The Country Squire, I thought, "What a wonderful place for a rendezvous." A blazing fire welcomed my chilled bones as the fragrance of apples in a barrel greeted my nostrils. I was seated in a country, cozy log cabin room that has a big fat tree growing through the center of it. The tree has a cushioned bench surrounding its trunk.

You can't imagine how good the Squire's clam chowder tasted on that chilly day. Being as faithful to my diet as possible, I also had an asparagus salad with a pot of hot English tea. I would have loved a glass of wine, especially since I had just passed the Duplin Winery; but no, the Squire is in a dry county. So if you think you might be so inclined, be sure to bring your alcoholic beverages with you.

Although the Squire does a fantastic Crab Louise and Shrimp Fritcheg for dinner, it is best known for its "mood cooking with an Asian accent." The Korean Barbecued Beef and Kailua Steak are absolutely outstanding. Also not to be missed is the Squire's brown rice. Any of the broiled steaks and seafood should get your diet's okay, but if you request in advance, the Squire can accommodate most any requirements.

After touring the Squire's various dining rooms, all of which have an English flavor, I decided that the Baronial Hall was most impressive. It features its original wide plank floors, tables suspended from the ceiling with heavy chains, and the portrait of Baron Gilbert De Clair. Although no actual testing was done when the late parapsychologist from Duke University, Dr. J. B. Rhine, visited the Squire, he is said to have believed that the Baronial Hall was inhabited by spirits. If so, I don't blame them for not wanting to leave this warm and festive habitat.

Not only is the Squire's interior inviting, but many of the rooms' diamond-shaped windows look out on beautiful gardens. Paths wind their way among tall pine and oak trees where the design has disturbed as little of nature as possible.

The Country Squire is located on N. C. 24, five miles east of Warsaw. Lunch is served from 11:30 a. m. to 2:00 p. m., and dinner from 5:30 to 9:30 p. m. daily. For reservations call (919) 296–1727.

THE COUNTRY SQUIRE'S
KAILUA STEAK

3 ribeye steaks
⅜ cup soy sauce
2 teaspoons sesame oil
½ clove garlic, minced
2¼ teaspoons sugar
1 teaspoon chopped
   fresh chives or onion
about 6 scallions

1 egg
1 teaspoon any type oil
⅓ cup milk
3 tablespoons flour
sesame seeds
oil for deep frying
seedless grapes or
   mandarin oranges

Cut steaks into ¼-inch strips. Mix soy sauce, sesame oil, garlic, sugar, and chives in a 2-cup container and add water to fill. Cover steak with mixture and marinate in refrigerator for 24 hours.

Alternate strips of meat and scallions between two skewers, piercing each onion and strip of meat on both ends. Make a batter of egg, 1 teaspoon oil, milk, and flour. Dip beef and onion in batter, then roll in sesame seeds to coat. Deep fry until light brown. Remove skewers, top with grapes or orange slices, and serve with sweet and sour sauce (see recipe below). Serves 4.

THE COUNTRY SQUIRE'S
SWEET AND SOUR SAUCE

juice of two lemons
1 small green pepper,
   chopped
½ to ¾ cup water

¾ cup light brown sugar
¾ tablespoon or more
   cornstarch
1 teaspoon vinegar

Combine all ingredients in a saucepan and cook until sauce is thick and green pepper is tender.

THE COUNTRY SQUIRE'S QUAIL PIE

1 small guinea hen
4 quail, parboiled
1 recipe corn bread,
    crumbled
¾ cup chopped onions

¾ cup chopped
    green peppers
1 cup chopped mushrooms
1 cup chopped celery
6 to 8 strips bacon

Boil hen until meat falls off the bone, about 1½ hours. Set stock aside. After hen has cooled, debone it and mince the meat. Sauté onions, peppers, mushrooms, and celery. Add vegetables and minced hen to crumbled corn bread, and moisten with enough stock to allow the mixture to be kneaded to a loose consistency. Place mixture in greased casserole dish and top with quail; backs of quail should be pressed into the corn bread mixture, but breasts should show. Crisscross strips of bacon across tops of quail, and cook at 350 degrees for 50 minutes.

Serve with egg gravy (see recipe below). Serves 4.

THE COUNTRY SQUIRE'S EGG GRAVY

1 cup chopped onions
1 cup chopped celery
1 clove garlic, crushed
2 tablespoons butter
1 cup stock from guinea hen

2 to 3 tablespoons flour
½ teaspoon fennel seed
salt and pepper
3 boiled eggs, chopped
1 scallion, chopped

Sauté onions, garlic, and celery in butter. Add enough stock to the flour to make a smooth paste, and stir it into the vegetables. Stir in remainder of stock and add spices and egg. Top with scallions before serving. Serves 4.

THE FRENCH COUNTRY INN, LTD.
Selma

THE FRENCH COUNTRY INN, LTD.

Even when I was a little girl I noticed that French cooking was mentioned with hushed tones of awe. When I visited the French Country Inn, Ltd., I asked the owner and chef, Phillip Forman, to explain why French cuisine has received that reputation of superiority. "Because," he replied, "we operate as an art form. This art form is carried through not only in the composition of the menu but in the presentation to the customer who has acquired a taste for this art form."

The inn is housed in a beautiful turn-of-the-century Georgian-style mansion. If offers a fixed menu consisting of courses particular to a single French province. The same menu is continued for two weeks and is then completely changed to represent another province.

The evening I dined at the inn, the cuisine was from Bretagne, and this explanation was printed on the menu: "Brittany is the French province most dominated by the sea. It lies in the northwest of France, a peninsula tempered by the harsh nature of the land. The cuisine is rich in seafood, dairy, and the lighter meats. Bretons are truly provincial in manner being of Celtic origin and independent in their attitudes and language. Simplicity is the manner in the Breton life and cuisine."

Apparently, simplicity has an entirely different connotation for the French than for me. The cauliflower potage in cream and chicken stock tantalized my palate. The delicious Brittany scallops and salad were followed by stuffed veal in an apple cider sauce. Each dish was savored with a white Muscadet wine from the Loire Valley.

Sound simple so far? It was simply elegant, as was the dessert. Just a simple almond pastry filled with strawberries, raspberries, and brandy, and topped with custard and whipped cream. You would be hard put to stay on a diet, but a day or so of starvation afterwards would be worth your experience at this tastefully appointed restaurant.

The French Country Inn, Ltd., is located at 309 West Railroad Street in Selma. Seating hours are from 7:00 to 8:30 p. m. Wednesday through Saturday. For reservations call (919) 965–5229.

THE FRENCH COUNTRY INN'S
TERRINE DE POISSON
(Fish Pâté)

1 pound fillets of whiting or flounder	1 egg yolk
1 pound salmon	1 tablespoon chopped parsley
4 tablespoons butter	salt and pepper
1 cup fine bread crumbs	mace
¼ cup milk	cayenne pepper

Chop fillets very fine and combine with 2 tablespoons softened butter, bread crumbs, egg, milk, and parsley. Mix well and season highly with salt and pepper. Free salmon steak of skin and bones and cut in narrow strips. Put a ½-inch layer of fish mixture on the bottom of a small, round terrine mold. Place a layer of fish strips over this. Sprinkle with salt, pepper, a dash of mace, and a dash of cayenne. Continue this process until terrine is tightly packed. Dot the top layer with butter and cover tightly with aluminum foil. Bake at 300 degrees for 2½ hours. Do not take foil off until terrine is chilled.

Unmold and garnish with parsley. Serves 8 to 10.

THE FRENCH COUNTRY INN'S
JAMBON A LA POELE
(Ham in White Wine Sauce)

6 to 8 thin slices uncooked ham	1 cup dry white wine (Chablis, Riesling, or Muscadet)
2 tablespoons butter	salt and pepper
2 tablespoons flour	

Melt butter in frying pan. When butter is sizzling hot, brown ham slices on both sides. Allow 5 minutes for cooking ham. Remove ham, stir in flour, moisten with white wine, and stir as sauce thickens. Season with only a little salt, as the ham may be quite salty. Add a dash of fresh pepper.

Place slices of ham on a warm platter. Pour the sauce over the ham and garnish with sprigs of parsley. Serves 3 to 4.

THE FRENCH COUNTRY INN'S
MOUSSE AU CHOCOLAT
(Chocolate Mousse)

4 1-ounce squares baking chocolate
¼ cup water

¾ cup sugar
5 eggs
1 tablespoon cognac

Melt chocolate in top of double boiler. Add water and sugar; stir until sugar is dissolved. Separate egg yolks from whites. Add yolks one by one, beating vigorously. Remove from the heat and add cognac. Beat egg whites stiff and fold into chocolate mixture. Pour into individual molds or a dessert bowl and refrigerate.

Let it stand for at least 12 hours. The longer it stands the better it is. This mousse keeps well for several days. Serves 4 to 6.

THE ANGUS BARN
Raleigh

THE ANGUS BARN If grassroots America of the early part of the century were described, mention would be made of old country barns, Mom churning butter, Dad bringing in logs, children stringing popcorn at Christmas, and the unmistakable aroma of apple pie greeting you at the kitchen door. These are some of the things that today's children read about but old-timers remember.

The feelings of an earlier time can be rekindled at The Angus Barn. This is partly because the building is an assemblage of ancient barns and dwellings. In the Angus Tavern area, for instance, sturdy old log beams blend with the cobblestones covering the floor to create a warm, rustic decor. The stones were actually ballast tossed shoreside from anchored ships in the Charleston harbor, but the restaurant's other stone floors were rescued from dismantled slave quarters in Johnston County.

Surrounding one of the main dining rooms is a balcony replicating a loft, complete with hay, pitchforks, and antique farm tools. To complete the homespun atmosphere, the waitresses are costumed in calico aprons and caps, an attire that recalls certain maternal memories.

The bar features a marble counter top from one of the area's stately old hotels. Its base is constructed from beautiful solid oak doors that once served as the entrance to the hotel's bedrooms. Ah, if only those doors could talk, what stories would be heard!

During the Christmas holidays, a whiff of nostalgia is bound to stir anyone who sees the Barn's gigantic Christmas trees trimmed in the style of the early part of the century, but of course the architecture and the food make dining a meaningful experience at any time.

The restaurant's nostril-tingling barbecued spareribs amply fulfill their aromatic promise. The shrimp cocktail is a surprise: The shrimp, from the coast of Spain, are so large that they are often mistaken for baby lobsters. Of course, the Barn is famed for its beef, and no one could be disappointed in the variety or quality of the Barn's steaks. They overload the star category with a selection including Chateaubriand, Filet Mignon, beef kabobs, and beef and lobster combinations. In the seafood department, the Barn not only does very special preparations with shrimp scampi, scallops, and flounder for their regular patrons, but they also work with Duke Medical Center's rice diet patients, adhering to the diet's strict requirements for food preparations.

The Barn also has a refreshing philosophy which stipulates that the best wine to buy is the wine that suits you best. The beer and wine selection accommodates modestly priced wines as well as a 1959 Château Lafite-Rothschild. The Barn's dessert tray features a broad variety of freshly baked pies (yes, apple, too), but a pleasant, light delicacy after a scrumptious entrée is the Raspberry Grand Marnier, a sherbet parfait.

Before departing this tasty dose of Americana at her best, stop at the country store, where an antique refrigerator offers many of the Barn's specialties, including the famous barbecue sauce.

The Angus Barn is located on U. S. 70 west at Airport Road in Raleigh. Dinner is served from 5:30 to 11:30 p. m. Monday through Saturday, and from 5:30 to 10:00 p. m. on Sundays. For reservations call (919) 787–3505.

ANGUS BARN'S STUFFED POTATOES

6 large Idaho potatoes	1 tablespoon chopped
1 stick butter	chives
3½ tablespoons grated	1 teaspoon salt
Parmesan cheese	½ teaspoon black pepper
2 tablespoons finely	⅛ teaspoon monosodium
crumbled cooked bacon	glutamate
1 tablespoon sour cream	paprika

Grease potatoes and bake at 400 degrees for 45 minutes. Cut in half lengthwise. Spoon out centers while hot and put in mixing bowl. Save the skins.

51

Combine all remaining ingredients except paprika, then add to spooned-out potato. Mix with electric mixer for 3 minutes at medium speed. Place mixture in potato skins. Sprinkle lightly with paprika. Brown in hot oven approximately 4 minutes. Serves 8 to 12.

ANGUS BARN'S RASPBERRY GRAND MARNIER

1 quart raspberry sherbet	16 strawberries
½ cup raspberry preserves	2 ounces Grand Marnier
½ cup white wine	grated peel of ½ orange

Combine raspberry preserves with white wine, blending well. Spoon two scoops of raspberry sherbet into each of 4 parfait glasses. Pour wine and preserves over sherbet. Place 4 strawberries in each glass and pour ½ ounce Grand Marnier over strawberries. Add a sprinkle of orange peel and serve. Serves 4.

ANGUS BARN'S CHOCOLATE CHESS PIE

1⅓ sticks butter	3 small eggs
1⅓ squares unsweetened chocolate	⅓ teaspoon salt
	1 teaspoon vanilla
1⅓ cups sugar	1 9-inch pie crust, unbaked

Melt butter and chocolate over boiling water. Mix sugar, eggs, salt, and vanilla; add to chocolate mixture. Pour into pie shell and bake at 375 degrees for about 35 minutes.

SUDI'S
Durham

SUDI'S

Sudi's is endowed with two distinct personalities in one setting, primarily because it presents two separate restaurants in one building. The upstairs restaurant, which maintains a casual image, serves lunch and lighter dinners. The downstairs, which is entered from the rear of the building, is more sophisticated and is open only for dinner.

I was happy to see that this 1893 building, which is the only remaining nineteenth-century structure still standing in downtown Durham, has retained its original gray brick Romanesque Revival facade, including the copper flame finial atop a dormer window. Like so many of North Carolina's restaurants in historical settings, Sudi's did not begin as a restaurant. Originally it was the W. A. Slater Company's store for men's clothing, and then it became Baldwin's, also a clothing store. The area downstairs is in existence because Baldwin's once needed additional space. It took one worker, one blind mule with a drag pan, and one year to dig out the basement.

Having descended to Sudi's lower dining quarters, I was intrigued with the exceptional wine list, which includes wines that are difficult to obtain elsewhere. My choice of entrée was not at all difficult. The Trout Imperial, which is broiled in dry vermouth and lemon juice, then topped with crabmeat sauce and garnished with caviar, seemed to leap right off the menu. I was glad that I followed my intuition, because the Mediterranean cuisine of Sudi's more than equaled my mental imagery.

In an effort to be "good," I chose to go upstairs and to be entertained with the weekend jazz ensemble instead of dessert. I read somewhere that you can cut your calorie temptations by redirecting your activities. It worked; and had I gone on a Thursday night, I could have worked off a calorie binge by joining in the clogging or square dancing.

My daughter Daintry, who weighs in at ninety-eight pounds wringing wet, tells me that her favorite lunch upstairs is the

Summer Reuben, which her figure can afford. For those of us whose bathroom scales scream obscenities, Sudi's offers the Scarsdale Diet for both lunch and dinner.

Sudi's is located at 111 West Main Street in Durham. Lunch is served from 11:30 a. m. to 2:30 p. m. Monday through Friday; dinner is served from 6:00 to 9:00 p. m. Monday through Wednesday, and until 10:00 p. m. Thursday through Saturday. For reservations call (919) 688–3664.

SUDI'S TROUT IMPERIAL

4 6-ounce trout fillets	salt and pepper
12 ounces fresh back-fin crabmeat	cayenne pepper
	1 cup heavy cream
2 tablespoons butter	5 egg whites
¼ cup dry vermouth	2 teaspoons lemon juice
4 teaspoons flour	black caviar for garnish

In a small skillet, sauté crabmeat in butter and vermouth, adding flour, salt, and cayenne to taste. Blend thoroughly, adding cream. Cook until crab is the consistency of deviled crab. Beat egg whites until they form stiff peaks. Broil trout 2 to 3 minutes, but not until "done." Combine lemon juice and salt and pepper, and pour over fish; cover with crab, top with egg whites, and bake at 500 degrees for 2 to 5 minutes. Garnish with caviar. Serves 4.

SUDI'S SUMMER REUBEN

2 slices Jewish rye bread	1 to 2 tablespoons coleslaw
Russian dressing	1 slice Swiss cheese
4 ounces sliced turkey	1 tablespoon butter

Spread Russian dressing over both pieces of bread. Add turkey, coleslaw, and Swiss cheese. Melt butter in a skillet and fry sandwich evenly on both sides. Serves 1.

SUDI'S CHICKEN SUPRÉMES POMMERY

4 deboned chicken breasts
½ cup flour
salt
2 tablespoons butter
1½ cups heavy cream

4 level tablespoons
  Pommery mustard
2 teaspoons fresh dill or
  1 teaspoon dry dill

Pound chicken to ¼-inch thick.

Dredge in salted flour and sauté in butter on both sides. Remove chicken from skillet and keep warm. Mix cream, mustard, and dill in skillet; boil to reduce cream. When thick, remove from heat and pour over chicken. Serves 4.

COLONIAL INN
Hillsborough

COLONIAL INN

When I step from the veranda onto the two-hundred-year-old wide planked floors of the Colonial Inn, I am proud of the quick thinking of our foremother, Sarah Stroud. Besieged by General Sherman's bummers, who were ransacking her inn, that valiant widow lady ran upstairs and waved her husband's Masonic apron from the balcony. Luckily the flag's symbol captured the eye of a sergeant who was a Mason. He ordered his soldiers to return their lootings to the inn.

Say what you will, I believe that symbol, which stood for finer values, stirred the sergeant to uphold a tradition. Who knows, had he not intervened, this venerable old inn might have ended in ashes. Perhaps Sarah could have rebuilt the inn, as it had been rebuilt in 1768 when the original tavern was destroyed by fire, but that is a thought I am glad needs no pondering.

The Colonial Inn continues today to stand for those same traditions of finer values that Mrs. Stroud was determined to preserve. I speak not only of the craftsmanship that was born from the ethic of building structures to last; I include the cooks' expertise in preparing the aristocracy of Southern cooking.

Amidst the friendliness that adds something special to the intimate dining rooms, you may enjoy fried chicken, country ham, or fresh seafood. This is Southern-style cooking that is not over-cooked, over-salted, or over-greasy, as unfortunately is often the case.

However, the Colonial Inn's manager, Pete Thompson, told me honestly that the fare is not for dieters, and for the most part he is correct. My calorie count tilted when I ate everything on a plate filled with country ham, potatoes, hot biscuits, and red eye gravy, all of which I embellished with half a bottle of Beaujolais. However, you could—yes, you could—diet with the broiled fresh flounder or ribeye steak and a tossed salad. You would have to pass up the apple cobbler or black walnut pie, as I did, but my feeling is that you need not pass up the Colonial Inn because you're trying to trim.

The Colonial Inn is located at 153 West King Street in Hillsborough. Lunch is served from 11:30 a. m. to 2:30 p. m., and dinner from 5:00 to 9:00 p. m., Monday through Saturday. On Sunday, family-style serving is from 11:30 a. m. to 9:00 p. m. For reservations call (919) 732–2461.

COLONIAL INN'S CORNWALLIS YAMS

6 medium sweet potatoes
1½ cups milk
1 cup sugar
½ cup crushed pineapple
1 stick butter
3 eggs, beaten

½ teaspoon salt
½ teaspoon ground
  cinnamon
½ teaspoon ground nutmeg
½ cup flaked coconut

Wash sweet potatoes and place in a large saucepan; cover with water and bring to a boil. Cover pan and simmer about 30 minutes. Peel and mash the potatoes. Add all remaining ingredients except coconut and mix well. Pour into a greased 13- by 9- by 2-inch baking dish. Bake at 350 degrees for 45 minutes. Sprinkle with coconut. Serves 12 to 14.

COLONIAL INN'S
GREEN BEANS AMANDINE

2 pounds fresh green beans
1 small ham hock
3 tablespoons butter

⅓ cup minced onion
⅔ cup sliced almonds
1 tablespoon salt

Remove strings from green beans. Cut beans into 1½-inch pieces and wash thoroughly. Place in a 5-quart Dutch oven and add the ham hock and water to cover. Bring to a boil and reduce heat. Cover and simmer for 1 hour. Drain off excess liquid. Sauté onions and almonds in butter until onions are transparent. Add beans and salt. Toss lightly. Serves 8.

COLONIAL INN'S BAKED APPLES

6 large baking apples
6 tablespoons sugar
1½ teaspoons ground
  cinnamon
1½ teaspoons ground
  nutmeg

2 tablespoons butter
½ to ¾ cup apple juice
red food coloring (optional)

Peel and core apples and place in a shallow 2-quart casserole. Pour 1 tablespoon sugar into the hole of each apple. Sprinkle each with cinnamon and nutmeg and top with 1 teaspoon butter. Heat apple juice to boiling and add red food coloring; pour juice into casserole. Bake uncovered at 400 degrees for 50 to 60 minutes, or until tender. Brush occasionally with juice. Serves 6.

THE VILLA TÉO
Chapel Hill

THE VILLA TÉO   Years ago, when I first walked down the columned garden path and stepped inside The Villa Téo, I felt as though I had entered a frame of one of those old forties movies. I became Ingrid Bergman appearing on the balcony through a Moorish arch, my eyes sweeping the room before dramatically descending the carved staircase. Pausing a moment on the second landing, I saw a cigarette lighter's flame expose the face of my contact. He was standing beside the fountain of the Greek goddess Aphrodite. The light from the dark stained glass played across his features as a menu slipped discreetly from his fingers and became wedged among the foliage of a tropical plant.

Alone, I chose a corner beneath a group of Portuguese tiles. Within moments, a European-trained waiter handed me a menu. Unmistakably, my contact's sign was written beside the entry for Courvoisier cognac. Trying to keep my nerves and figure supple, I chose the artichoke vinaigrette and Crepes Fitzgerald; but out of the corner of my eye, I noted that my confident contact had not only made a ribeye steak disappear, but was now ordering the almond cheesecake. I ate my meal and slowly sipped my champagne until my waiter suggested cognac. Not moving my head, I saw my contact swirl his cognac and inhale the bouquet. At that signal, I crossed through the Italian tavern room, up the stairs, and into the gallery.

As I complimented the proprietor, Bibi Danziger, on my excellent meal and the service, I noticed that the contact was pretending to study a fifteenth-century tapestry. I moved down the gallery of paintings, sculpture, and priceless furniture, and stopped at a massive antique German cupboard. Extracting the information tucked behind one of the twelve carved apostles, I heard the diversion the contact was creating to protect me. In a loud voice he was asking Mrs. Danziger if it were true that the Villa's architect, Gerard Tempesta, had opened the Villa with a fanfare of harpists, trumpeteers, and a cloud of white doves. Chuckling, she said she remembered not only the flamboyant celebration, but also the conduct of those doves, which was inappropriate for the occasion.

Outside once again, I awoke to realize that my imagined contact had no greater significance than that of a passing stranger. I have no date with destiny, only the fantasy that this incredible restaurant, assembled with materials from nineteenth-century mansions, had allowed me to create for a few adventurous hours.

The Villa Téo is located at 1213 East Franklin Street in Chapel Hill. It is open only for Sunday brunch, which is served from 11:00 a.m. to 2:00 p.m. For reservations call (919) 942–2266.

THE VILLA TÉO'S RED SALMON PÂTÉ

7 ¾-ounce cans North Pacific Salmon

1 8-ounce package cream cheese, softened

2 tablespoons chili sauce

2 tablespoons chopped parsley

2 tablespoons finely minced onion

¼ teaspoon Tabasco

Blend all ingredients. Mold and chill at least three hours. Serve with crackers. Serves 8.

THE VILLA TÉO'S
POPPY SEED DRESSING

¼ to ½ cup chopped onion

¾ cup tarragon vinegar

2 tablespoons vegetable oil

1 tablespoon sugar

1 teaspoon salt

1 teaspoon dry mustard

½ tablespoon poppy seed

¾ cup vegetable oil

Combine all ingredients except oil in electric blender. Blend well. Slowly add oil while machine is still blending. When thick, pour into jar with tight-fitting lid. Chill.

Shake before serving. Serves 8 to 10.

THE VILLA TÉO'S
CRAB CAKES SUPREME

1 pound crabmeat
2 slices very dry bread
1 medium onion
1 stick butter

1 teaspoon dry mustard
salt and pepper
1 egg

Grate bread and mix with crabmeat. Sauté onion in 1 table-spoon butter, then add to crabmeat. Stir in mustard, salt and pepper, egg, and 2 tablespoons butter. Mix and mold into cakes. Fry in butter until quite brown.

Serve piping hot. Serves 4.

THE VILLA TÉO'S
CREPES FITZGERALD

Filling:
8 ounces cream cheese
juice of 1 lemon
3 tablespoons sugar

1½ cups sour cream
rind of 1 lemon
vanilla (optional)

Sauce:
½ cup frozen orange juice
3 tablespoons butter, melted
3 teaspoons water (more or less depending
on desired thickness)

See Index for crepes recipe.

Blend ingredients for filling until smooth. Cool.

Blend ingredients for sauce until smooth. Heat to warm through. Fill a hot crepe with 3 tablespoons filling and top with sauce. Yields 25 crepes.

THE FEARRINGTON HOUSE
Chapel Hill

THE FEARRINGTON HOUSE

After traveling south for about eight miles on U.S. 15–501 from Chapel Hill, you'll look to your left and feel as if you'd stumbled upon a Southern Grandma Moses painting. An old dairy barn and silo sit beyond a lush green meadow. This is one of the soothing views available to the guests of The Fearrington House, a restaurant in a traditional white Colonial home.

When my friend and I visited the restaurant for Sunday brunch, we sat on a brick-floored back porch. We had two appealing views: one of the restaurant's herb garden, the harvest of which is used in the food preparations, and another of a large rose garden. The rose garden presents the perfect backdrop for the white latticework patio used during warm weather.

No detail has been spared by Fearrington's owner and decorator, Jenny Fitch. Her deft hand has made each of the twelve dining rooms of the restaurant into a tasteful blend of color and comfort. I adored the relaxed country feel of chintz and cotton print lounges sitting behind the wooden tables. Each table was covered with matching laminated prints and was accented with home-grown flowers. The flowers were displayed in such imaginative containers as bird cages and vases covered in broom straw, which lent a piquant charm to the pastoral setting.

A pleasing atmosphere always adds an extra measure to my meal. My brunch was no exception. It featured a dish of cold shrimp, scallops, and vegetables that was as pretty to look at as it was appetizing. A perfect for dieting, if you can refrain from dipping into the mayonnaise sauce. My friend enjoyed the vegetarian ratatouille plate. Best of all is the bourbon pecan pie, but my friend said that her lemon chess pie was a close second.

The most popular entrée for evening dining is veal in Madeira sauce with asparagus, or roast duck with lingonberry sauce. Special diets can be accommodated if the restaurant is given twenty-four hours notice. And before I forget, The

Fearrington House is in a dry county, so you must bring your own alcoholic beverages.

After brunch we enjoyed walking through the grape arbor at the rear of the house and visiting the studio of Jim Pringle, a potter. The Fitches plan to recycle the old dairy barn by making it a country market. There shoppers will find flowers, vegetables, and the wares of the craftsmen who are converting the old silo and other outbuildings on the Fearrington estate into working studios. This conversion will give even sharper punctuation to the Grandma Moses landscape.

The Fearrington House is eight miles south of Chapel Hill on U.S. 15–501. Dinner is served from 6:00 to 10:00 p.m. Wednesday through Saturday, and Sunday brunch is served from 11:30 a.m. to 2:00 p.m. For reservations call (919) 967–7770.

THE FEARRINGTON HOUSE'S
ROAST PORK LOIN

1 whole pork loin	2 tablespoons rosemary
1 cup brown sugar	1 tablespoon garlic powder
1 cup Plochmann's mustard	2 teaspoons salt
2 tablespoons sage	½ teaspoon pepper.

Split and debone pork loin. Blend other ingredients together and rub half over inside of pork. Tie meat securely with string. Rub remaining mixture over outside of pork. Roast at 350 degrees until an internal temperature of 155 degrees is reached.

Serve with mustard butter (see recipe below). Serves 4 to 6.

THE FEARRINGTON HOUSE'S
MUSTARD BUTTER

¼ pound butter, softened	4 tablespoons Plochmann's
½ clove garlic, pressed	mustard
juice of ½ lemon	

Whip butter until soft. Whip in remaining ingredients.

THE FEARRINGTON HOUSE'S
BOURBON PECAN PIE

Pastry:

1 cup plus 2 tablespoons
all-purpose flour
pinch of salt
½ stick butter

2 tablespoons vegetable
shortening
¼ cup cold water

Filling:

3 eggs
½ teaspoon salt
1 cup light Karo syrup

1 cup sugar
1 tablespoon bourbon
1 cup chopped pecan pieces

For the pastry, add the shortening and butter to the flour and salt, and work the mixture with fingertips until it resembles corn flakes. Blend in the water until all the ingredients can be worked into a ball. Chill. Roll out dough and fit into a 9-inch pie pan. Fill with pie weights or dry beans to keep the sides from collapsing, and bake at 425 degrees for 5 minutes. Remove from oven and lower temperature to 350 degrees.

Mix all ingredients for filling and pour into the shell. Bake for 45 to 60 minutes or until the pie is firm to the touch.

Serve with freshly whipped cream or homemade vanilla ice cream. Serves 6.

RESTAURANT LA RÉSIDENCE
Chapel Hill

**RESTAURANT
LA RÉSIDENCE**

I'd venture to say few people know that the favorite dish of Dean Smith is veal kidneys. The management of La Résidence knows; each time the famed basketball coach of the University of North Carolina makes a reservation, the supply of kidneys is checked so that there will be no disappointment to the frequent guest. I imagine that even without the kidneys most diners would be hard pressed to find a source of disappointment in the restaurant's continental cuisine prepared with the classic French techniques.

French cooking seems at first a bit incongruous in a building constructed in 1926 as a Baptist rectory, but the interior has been stylishly decorated in a "country French" motif. Each dining room presents a unique personality, ranging from a casual look with blackeyed susans in an earthenware pitcher set upon a primitive antique sideboard, to a more sophisticated room dressed in a rich verdant color scheme. This room's fabric-covered banquettes are supplied with comfortably squashy pillows that present an invitation to lounge about as you might picture yourself in a chic Parisian salon.

La Résidence's cold blueberry soup was a crisply refreshing way to begin a meal after a hot summer day. The restaurant serves a continually evolving repertoire of enticing dishes, but one bite of the Filet Mignon with Raifort Sauce convinced me that at least one item will remain on the menu as a staple. It certainly will be a staple in my household. The *nouvelle cuisine* is lighter than the usual French fare, but if you are truly trying to de-escalate your calorie intake, the chefs will be happy to poach or broil a number of special dishes with wine and herbs.

The wine list offers a carefully chosen selection of both imported and domestic vintages, plus a small but adequate selection of imported beers.

When I asked about the restaurant's marvelous Espresso Ice Cream, I was told that the base recipe came originally from *Food & Wine* magazine but had gradually evolved into an entirely new taste. You can imagine the chef's surprise when *Food & Wine* passed along a reader's request for the recipe for La Résidence's ice cream. Naturally, the restaurant was only too pleased to share its success, which may be part of the reason La Résidence has been highly acclaimed by not only *Food & Wine*, but *Fortune* and *Holiday* magazines. The restaurant has won the Travel-Holiday Award four times. You may be sure that it is an award winner in my travels.

La Résidence is located at 220 West Rosemary Street in Chapel Hill. Dinner is served daily from 6:00 to 9:00 p.m., and Sunday brunch from 11:00 a.m. to 2:00 p.m. For reservations call (919) 967-2565.

LA RÉSIDENCE'S COLD BLUEBERRY SOUP

2 pints fresh blueberries
¼ bottle Beaujolais wine
1 10-ounce bottle apricot
　nectar
grated peel of 2 lemons

½ tablespoon coarse black
　pepper
pinch of salt
1 cup sour cream
¼ pint sliced strawberries

Put blueberries through a sieve or food mill. Add Beaujolais, apricot nectar, lemon peel, and salt and pepper. Stir and chill.

Garnish each bowl of soup with a generous dollop of sour cream and sliced strawberries. Serves 6.

LA RÉSIDENCE'S FILET MIGNON WITH SAUCE RAIFORT

6 to 8 beef fillets
1 pound unsalted butter
½ cup fresh chives, minced

5 tablespoons prepared
　horseradish
3 tablespoons lemon juice

4 garlic cloves, pressed

With electric mixer cream butter and mix in chives, horseradish, lemon juice, and garlic. Blend well. Cover bowl and refrigerate until firm.

Broil meat slightly on both sides; place a generous dollop

of butter on each fillet and broil until butter melts. Use left-over sauce for other grilled meats and fresh vegetables. Serves 8.

LA RÉSIDENCE'S PORK WITH MUSTARD SAUCE

6 half-inch boned pork loin chops
¼ cup or more Wondra flour
1 tablespoon dry mustard
3 tablespoons butter
3 tablespoons lemon juice
4 tablespoons brandy
⅓ cup Pommery mustard
1 cup heavy cream
salt and pepper to taste
6 cornichon pickles
½ pound cooked fettucine

Lightly coat the pork with a mixture of the flour and dry mustard. Sauté the pork in butter over a medium to high heat until lightly brown on each side. Add the prepared mustard, cream, and salt and pepper. Stir the sauce until it is hot, then add the pork and cook slowly over a low heat until thoroughly cooked. Serve with hot fettucine and garnish with cornichons. Serves 6.

LA RÉSIDENCE'S ESPRESSO ICE CREAM

1 ¾ cups half and half
2 tablespoons instant coffee
9 egg yolks
⅛ teaspoon salt
¾ cup sugar
1 ½ cups whipping cream
6 tablespoons unsalted butter
1 tablespoon vanilla
¼ cup ground espresso coffee

Mix half and half with instant coffee and scald in small saucepan. Beat egg yolks with salt in large bowl, gradually adding sugar until mixture is light and fluffy. Slowly add half and half, beating constantly. Transfer to heavy saucepan and cook over medium heat, stirring, until mixture thickens. Do not let mixture boil. Blend in cream and butter, and let cool.

Stir in vanilla. Strain. Pour into ice cream freezer and churn until desired consistency. Fold in espresso. Allow to set up in freezer at least 30 minutes before serving. Yields 2 quarts.

THE MANOR INN
Pinehurst

THE MANOR INN Ⓘf you happen to be out bicycling in Pinehurst and find yourself in the mood for refreshment, The Manor Inn is one of the few places where you can expect your bicycle to be parked by the doorman. That was the discovery four young women made one Mother's Day. Though it was a busy day for the Manor, none of the unusual amenities were amiss.

Upon your arrival at this Southern landscaped filigree of dogwoods, you'll notice that the 1923 white stucco structure is accented by an abundance of red geraniums. They spill out of the window boxes from early spring through the fall. It is during these seasons that the rockers lining the front porch offer a beguiling invitation to sit and sip the Manor's "iced tea." The drink is an interesting alcoholic concoction that does not include tea. That minor infraction, according to the Manor's owner, Joe Grantham, has not deterred the drink's popularity in the least.

Inside the cozy interior are a number of dining options to suit one's choice of atmosphere or the time of day. For lunch I enjoyed the sun porch and, in particular, my meal of escargots. This is an ingenious appetizer-sandwich consisting of mushroom-stuffed snails nestled inside a Kaiser roll. You may, if you choose a simpler meal, have fresh fruit or shrimp salad with a light dessert.

Dinner at the Manor takes on a somewhat grander significance, with intricate ice carvings, silver champagne coolers, and six courses selected from a rotating menu. The cuisine is basically continental in style, with Oysters Rockefeller and stuffed shrimp commanding the most attention for appetizers. The entrées are split fairly evenly between classic French dishes and more standard fare as Filet Mignon, fried chicken, and baked ham. Desserts are similar in choice, ranging from lemon soufflé to apple pie.

If you are vacationing at the Manor, then you should also try the Yorkshire popovers for breakfast. After any meal you'll find that there is such a variety of recreation possibilities that you can work off any superfluous calories by swimming, golf, tennis, or the riding club's offering of tree-lined horse trails. Then you can come back for another sumptuous meal or maybe just collapse on the front porch with a glass of "iced tea."

The Manor Inn is located on Magnolia Road in Pinehurst. It is open throughout the year. Breakfast is served from 7:00 to 9:00 a. m., lunch from 11:30 a. m. to 2:00 p. m., and dinner from 6:30 to 8:30 p. m. For reservations call (919) 295–6176.

THE MANOR INN'S
FRIED STUFFED SHRIMP

12 to 15 large shrimp,
  butterflied
1 can water chestnuts
4 ounces Prosciutto ham

2 to 3 eggs
flour for dredging
oil for frying

Chop 3 or 4 shrimp and water chestnuts into paste. Spread this mixture on remainder of shrimp. Cover with Prosciutto ham. Dip in beaten egg and dredge in flour. Let dry on rack and slide into deep fat at 375 degrees and cook until golden brown. Serve with sweet and sour sauce (see Index). Serves 4 to 6.

THE MANOR INN'S
BAKED SMOKED HAM IN RYE DOUGH

1 smoked ham
½ cup brown sugar
1 small can crushed
  pineapple

mustard to coat ham
rye bread dough
  (see recipe below)

Coat ham with a layer each of mustard, brown sugar, and drained pineapple. Roll out dough and wrap around ham. Bake at 350 degrees for two hours.

Some say you should throw the ham away and eat the rye bread. Five-pound ham serves 10 to 12.

THE MANOR INN'S RYE BREAD

1 pint water, boiling
2 tablespoons butter
2 tablespoons sugar
1½ teaspoons salt
cold water

2 tablespoons dry
  active yeast
7 cups unbleached
  white flour
2½ cups rye flour

Combine boiling water, butter, sugar, and salt in a mixing bowl. Stir until butter melts; then add cold water and stir until mixture is lukewarm. Stir in yeast and let sit 5 minutes. Stir in 3 cups white flour and all the rye. Beat vigorously until smooth. Work in enough remaining flour to make a stiff dough. Then turn out onto a floured board and knead until smooth and satiny. Place dough in greased bowl, oil the top of the dough, cover with a cloth, and place in a warm spot to rise. Dough should double in bulk.

Punch down; shape half into a loaf to bake and wrap the remainder around the ham. After loaf has risen a second time, put in a greased 9- by 5- by 3-inch covered loaf pan, then bake at 350 degrees for about an hour.

THE MANOR INN'S ICED TEA

1 ounce gin
1 ounce rum
1½ ounces whiskey sour
  mix

½ ounce Triple Sec
1 ounce vodka
Coca-Cola
ice

Pour liquors and whiskey sour mix into an 8-ounce glass and shake. Fill glass with Coke and ice. Stir. Serves 1.

PINE CREST INN
Pinehurst

PINE CREST INN

As you drive through the towering pines and varied, lush plantings that characterize the Pinehurst of today, it is hard to imagine that this golfer's utopia was created out of a barren wilderness. The tract was nothing but leveled tree stumps when James G. Tufts bought it in 1895 and hired landscape architect Frederick Law Olmstead to design a resort for convalescents. If anyone could create a pleasant spot out of that land it was Olmstead, who had designed New York City's Central Park and the gardens of Biltmore House in Asheville.

Tufts led Pinehurst in a new direction entirely when he found his healthier patrons disturbing the cattle in his fields by hitting little white balls with clubs. Going against the common belief that golf was a passing fancy, Tufts built a nine-hole course. In 1900 Scottish golf pro Donald Ross arrived at Pinehurst and began designing more courses. The success of golf at Pinehurst earned international reputations for both Ross and the resort.

Ross eventually invested some of his earnings at Pinehurst by buying the 1913 Pine Crest Inn. He endowed the inn with a comfortable, sporty atmosphere that has remained intact since golfer Bob Barrett purchased Pine Crest in 1961.

I found that visiting the inn today is like slipping on an old shoe. There are no signs reading "No stuffy people allowed," because that isn't necessary. The stuffies couldn't withstand the inn's hearty camaraderie. I don't think it is possible to remain a stranger at Pine Crest for more than thirty minutes; some guest has either dragged you over to the bar and introduced you to everyone, or you're in a singalong around the piano.

After a long trip I was easily persuaded to try a Transfusion, an unlikely drink of vodka, Gatorade, and grape juice. It slipped down remarkably easily in the company of the inn's voluptuous little Gouda Puffs.

Luckily my group realized in time that we were about to miss dinner, so we settled down in the main dining room, which is decorated with cheerful wallpaper and crystal chandeliers. The cuisine at Pine Crest can best be described as pure Americana. The chef, Carl Jackson, has been with the inn for 49 years. He specializes in sincere cooking, such as fresh-squeezed orange juice for breakfast and "scratch" bran muffins, not to mention the best clam chowder I've had in this state.

Our meal began with a fresh crabmeat cocktail and a gentle Bordeaux from the Lichine vineyards. The wine was the exact prescription for my tremendous Filet Mignon served with tiny boiled potatoes, green beans al dente, and the tastiest fried zucchini to be found anywhere. I can hardly believe that I found room for my blueberry cream pie, which was served with a Cabernet. Then, because someone insisted that we finish the meal with a smooth drink called the Afterglow, we did. After two of those, you do glow!

The Pine Crest Inn offers a convivial atmosphere that lures you to sink down in one of the overstuffed chairs beside the fire and "set and joke a spell" while the world struggles along without you.

The Pine Crest Inn is located on Dogwood Road in Pinehurst. Breakfast is served from 7:00 to 9:00 a.m., and dinner from 7:00 to 9:00 p.m. For reservations call (919) 295-6121.

PINE CREST INN'S SIX WEEKS MUFFINS

3 cups Bran Buds	2 cups buttermilk
1¼ cups boiling water	2½ cups all-purpose flour
2 beaten eggs	2½ teaspoons soda
1½ cups sugar	1 teaspoon salt
½ cup vegetable oil	1 teaspoon cinnamon

Pour water over bran and set aside. In electric mixer beat eggs; add sugar, oil, and buttermilk one at a time, mixing thoroughly. Scrape sides with rubber spatula to incorporate ingredients. Pour into greased muffin tins, filling each cup a little more than half full. Bake at 375 degrees for about 30 minutes. For miniature tins, bake about 12 minutes. Yields 24 large muffins.

PINE CREST INN'S GOUDA PUFFS

1 ½-pound wheel Gouda
  cheese
1 package Pepperidge Farm
  crescent rolls

2 teaspoons caraway seeds
1 egg white

Split Gouda horizontally to make two thinner rounds. Divide crescent roll dough into squares and arrange around each circle of Gouda. Tuck pastry securely in place and sprinkle with caraway seeds. Place on greased cookie sheet with seam side down. Brush with egg white. Bake at 350 degrees for 15 to 25 minutes. Cut into bite-sized wedges and serve hot. Serves 4.

PINE CREST INN'S SPINACH AND MUSHROOM SALAD

1 pound fresh spinach
½ pound fresh mushrooms,
  stemmed
2 ripe avocadoes

Naturally Fresh Poppy Seed
  Dressing
¼ cup olive oil
⅓ package dry Ranch Herb
  Dressing

Wash spinach; stem and tear into bite-sized pieces. Place in plastic bag in refrigerator to crispen. Marinate mushrooms in Poppy Seed Dressing for an hour. Combine olive oil with herb dressing. Peel and slice avocadoes. Toss together spinach, herbs dressing, mushrooms, and avocadoes. Serves 6.

PINE CREST INN'S AFTERGLOW

1 ounce vodka
1 ounce Grand Marnier
1 ounce Bailey's Irish Cream

1 ounce Kahlua
2 ounces heavy cream
ice

Combine all ingredients in blender and blend until frothy. Serves 2.

THE ELMS
Greensboro

THE ELMS The Elms restaurant was born when its proprietor, Claudia Green, graduated with a master's degree in nutrition from the University of North Carolina at Greensboro. Her irritation at the fact that there was nowhere to eat in Greensboro on Sundays spurred Ms. Green to renovate a building that has housed many enterprises since it began as a hardware store in 1896. Long, tedious months produced the restoration of the building's original barrel-vaulted, sculptured tin ceiling. Preferring to complement antiquity with the contemporary, Ms. Green has effected an eclectic look with an airiness that gives the old building an upbeat atmosphere.

More important than the inviting setting, however, are the restaurant's inviting dishes. Even a five-year-old boy remarked that getting dressed up wasn't so bad when you could have The Elms's French toast. And no wonder, when you can enjoy classical music and freshly squeezed orange juice with the French toast, which is made with a brandy egg batter. Even the muffins and rolls are baked daily in the Fleur de Lis, the pastry shop behind the restaurant.

The motto of The Elms, "Once a customer, always a friend," was adopted from another business that occupied the premises, but it has been translated into a present-day reality. Out-of-towners now call ahead to book their favorite table. They know, as do local patrons, that they can order special dishes not on the menu, such as peanut soup. In fact, that's just what a circus did last year to honor its elephant, Bambi, on its birthday.

The Elms's chefs were trained in New Orleans, New York, and Paris. Dieters can take heart that the continental fare won't pass them by, however. The cooks take delight in cheating the calories but not your appetite by broiling fresh fish or chicken in a light wine sauce. Those who watch no calories can dine on Scallops Dill, Scampi Pernod, or a mouth-watering chicken stuffed with crabmeat. If you've sinned thus far, fudge a tad more with the Grasshopper Pie or Grand

Marnier Cheesecake. The Elms's superb cuisine offers an uncommon dining experience along with a wine cellar featuring first-quality imported and domestic wines.

The Elms is located at 223 South Elm Street in Greensboro. It is open from 7:00 a. m. to 10:00 p. m. seven days a week. My advice is not to miss the weekend brunches, which start at 8:30 a. m. Reservations are a must for dinner; call (919) 274–6776.

THE ELMS'S VEAL IN THE TREES

8 2-ounce escallops of veal
1½ cups sliced mushrooms
½ cup dry white wine
1 tablespoon chopped
  shallots
1 stick butter
flour for dredging
salt and pepper
strawberries
lemon wedges

Melt butter in each of two large pans. Dredge the veal in flour and drop into the butter. Sauté for one minute on each side. Add half of mushrooms to each pan and sauté for another minute. Add shallots and wine, and reduce liquid for 1 to 2 minutes. Dust with salt and pepper. Remove from pan and arrange on 4 plates.

Garnish with strawberries and lemon wedges. Serves 4.

THE ELMS'S FLEUR DE LIS
CHOCOLATE CHUNK COOKIES

2 sticks sweet butter
1 teaspoon salt
1 teaspoon vanilla
¾ cup granulated sugar
¾ cup light brown sugar
2 large eggs
2¼ cups all-purpose flour
1 teaspoon baking soda
1 teaspoon hot water
12 ounces semi-sweet
  chocolate, broken into
  nail-size chunks
1½ cups broken walnuts

Cream the butter; add salt, sugars, and vanilla. Add eggs and beat well. Add half the flour and mix at low speed. Beat until incorporated, but do not over-beat. Scrape the bowl. Dissolve soda in hot water; mix into the dough. Add the remaining flour, and beat to mix only. Stir in walnuts and chocolate chunks. Drop onto foil-lined cookie sheet, and bake at 350 degrees for 8 to 10 minutes.

Let cool before removing from foil. Yields 5 dozen.

THE ELMS'S FLEUR DE LIS
VIENNESE TRIANGLES

Pastry:

2 sticks unsalted butter
⅓ cup sugar
1 teaspoon vanilla
1 egg

2½ cups all-purpose flour, unsifted
⅓ cup raspberry apricot jam

Topping:

5 egg whites
1 cup sliced almonds
1½ cups sugar
3 tablespoons flour

1 tablespoon light corn syrup
1 teaspoon cinnamon
½ teaspoon almond extract

¼ teaspoon baking powder

Grease 10- by 15-inch jelly roll pan and set it aside. Cream butter with sugar. Add vanilla; beat in egg; blend in flour. Pat pastry evenly into pan; refrigerate one hour to let set.

Spread raspberry jam over entire surface of pastry. Position rack in lower third of oven and preheat to 350 degrees.

In 2½-quart saucepan, combine all ingredients for topping except extract and baking powder. Place over very low heat; stir constantly until mixture reaches 200 degrees. Remove from heat; stir in extract and baking powder. Pour over crust, spreading evenly. Bake until golden brown, about 30 minutes. Cool in pan on rack.

When cool, cut into 1½ inch squares, then cut each diagonally to make triangles. Yields 50.

THE DEPOT
High Point

THE DEPOT

Remember the old-timey railroad dining car, with its tuxedoed waiters, linen tablecloths, and fresh flowers? That memory will return when you step from the railway platform into High Point's two-story 1907 terminal, which has been converted to The Depot restaurant. The reconstruction has preserved the romance and sophistication of the dining car, with period furnishings on the mezzanine level and curtained booths with original wooden benches on the main floor. Running the height of both stories are arched windows encased in elaborately carved molding. I wondered if this window treatment had been borrowed from the Jarrett House Hotel, which originally occupied the location. It seems that prior to the 1848 railroad charter, Manliff Jarrett also operated a stagecoach line on the Plank Road. Just before arriving at High Point, the stagecoach driver advised Jarrett of his passenger load by giving a short blast on his horn for each person aboard.

Naturally, technology has replaced that old Plank Road, but as you dine, you may notice the vague vibrations of a train rumbling past the platform, reminding you of the exciting promises of train travel.

For lunch I had the Caesar salad, but did fudge a smidgen on my diet with a fresh-baked cheese roll. Then curiosity got the best of me, so I had a thimbleful of the white bean soup, which is made with a tangy tomato sauce and is delicious. I did forgo the praline sundae, even though the waiter promised that each sundae is blessed to remove all calories.

If you have a mouth that experiences taste, then Tournaedos Stanley is strongly recommended. It is a grilled fillet of beef with a voluptuous horseradish sauce. If dieting, you may prefer the Flounder Bercy, baked in a lemon and shallot sauce.

You will enjoy selecting a wine from the perfectly controlled, 55-degree wine cellar, which accommodates everything from inexpensive house wines to a five-hundred-dollar bottle of Château Lafite-Rothschild.

After you've enjoyed your meal prepared by the chef, Michael D'Atre, you will be presented with a complimentary cruet of pastel cigarettes or a choice of cigars ceremoniously prepared by a waiter schooled in this art.

You'll find a distinctly different mood if you visit the bar before or after dinner. It used to be the baggage room and has been decorated to retain that image. You might even pop in and have a drink before your conductor calls out "All aboard!"

The Depot is located at 400 High Street in High Point. Lunch is served from 11:30 a. m. to 2:00 p. m. Monday through Friday, and dinner from 6:00 to 10:00 p. m. Monday through Saturday. For reservations call (919) 883–1364.

THE DEPOT'S SHRIMP VICTORIA

48 shrimp, cleaned and deveined	salt and pepper
	¼ cup white wine
1 stick butter or margarine	½ cup sour cream

Sauce:

¾ stick butter or margarine	2 cups milk
⅜ cup flour	1 teaspoon basil
1 pint fish fumet (see recipe below)	2 spring onions, sliced
	1 cup fresh mushrooms

To make Victoria sauce, melt ¾ stick butter and add flour. Cook 4 minutes, until roux smells like hazelnuts. Add fish fumet and milk; cook 5 minutes, stirring frequently. Add basil, onions, and mushrooms; cook 3 minutes. Set aside for later use.

Foam remaining butter and add shrimp and salt and pepper; cover and sweat 1 minute. Add wine and sauté until liquid is reduced to half. Add Victoria sauce and simmer 2 minutes. Remove from heat and garnish with sour cream.

Serve immediately over rice pilaf. Serves 6 to 8.

THE DEPOT'S FISH FUMET

fish bones from 4 medium
  fish
1 fish head
2 tablespoons unsalted
  butter
1 gallon water

½ cup rough-cut onion
½ cup rough-cut celery
5 sprigs parsley
½ teaspoon whole
  peppercorns
1 small bay leaf

½ lemon, cut up

Sauté fish head and bones in butter, then add to water with all the seasonings and vegetables. Bring to a boil, then reduce heat and simmer for at least four hours. Remove from heat when liquid is reduced to ¼ of original.

Strain and use, or freeze in plastic jars. Yields 1 quart.

THE DEPOT'S RICE PILAF

½ stick butter
½ cup chopped onions
1 cup uncooked rice

2 cups chicken stock
  (see Index)
salt and pepper

Sauté onions in butter until transparent. Add rice and stock, and bring to a boil. Reduce heat to low and cover. Cook until all liquid is absorbed. Season to taste.

Fluff with a fork and serve hot. Serves 4.

SALEM TAVERN
Winston-Salem

SALEM TAVERN

No, George Washington never ate here. He did, however, sleep next door at the original Salem Tavern for two nights in 1791. I would imagine that he bypassed the "publick room" where the "ordinary" were served, and ate instead in the "gentlemen's room," which was located directly across the hall. Can't you just visualize one of your ancestors smoking a long clay pipe and rubbing shoulders—or more probably, lifting a tankard of ale—with the Father of Our Country?

Today, as you sit in a Windsor chair at a table set with pewter plates, the Tavern's waiters and waitresses in period costumes are certain to treat you with the same "kindness and cordiality" that was stipulated by the original Moravian elders. The Moravians, a devout Germanic people, immigrated to Pennsylvania to escape religious persecution in the 1730's. A segment of these methodical people migrated to North Carolina in 1753 and eventually built a planned community, keeping intact their strict code of morality. Records note that the brethren didn't frown on the use of spirits; it was the "deleterious influence of strangers" that caused them to limit the tavern, when they could, to "traveling strangers only." By the time of the Revolution, the tavern was famous throughout the Southeast for the high quality of its "entertainment," a term meaning, as it does today, "good food and drink taken amid hospitable surroundings." The tavern became so popular that by 1815 it was necessary to build the current tavern to house the overflow. It is in this tavern that you may dine beside a traditional Moravian fireplace or under a candle in a sconce that makes a flickering butterfly-shaped shadow against the foot-thick walls.

In the warmer months, my preference is the wisteria-cloaked arbor, where I always enjoy the chicken pie. If you are dieting, you might fancy a garden salad of spinach and mushrooms.

At dinner I am inclined toward Wiener Schnitzel or, if counting calories, the fresh rainbow trout sans stuffing. For dessert you'll never miss with the Tavern's cheesecake. My hips don't either, so I inhale only when the apple dumplings pass by. You may be refreshed by a wide selection of "spirits" that remain a part of the Tavern's hospitality.

When you visit Salem Tavern, set aside a day for seeing the restored village of Old Salem. You'll realize that Salem, whose name was taken from the Hebrew word meaning peace, continues to impart the same serene atmosphere as it did in yestertime.

Salem Tavern is located at 736 South Main Street in Winston-Salem. Lunch is served from 11:30 a. m. to 2:00 p. m., and dinner from 6:00 to 10:00 p. m., Tuesday through Sunday. For reservations call (919) 748–8585.

SALEM TAVERN'S HOLLANDAISE SAUCE

3 egg yolks, at room
  temperature
½ teaspoon salt
⅛ teaspoon cayenne pepper

2 tablespoons lemon juice
⅛ teaspoon salt
1½ sticks butter
½ cup sour cream

Combine egg yolks, lemon juice, salt, and cayenne in blender; blend, then let sit 4 to 5 minutes. Melt butter in a saucepan and pour slowly into blender. Add sour cream and blend again. Serve over cooked vegetables, such as fresh asparagus.

SALEM TAVERN'S WIENER SCHNITZEL HOLSTEIN

6 5- to 6-ounce veal
  cutlets
salt and pepper
2 cups flour
3 eggs
½ cup milk

2 cups dried bread crumbs
2 cups oil (¼ inch deep
  in pan)
6 fried eggs
anchovies
capers

The secret to a successful schnitzel is in the tenderizing of the veal. The cutlets should be pounded as thin as possible

91

with a meat mallet. Add salt and pepper to taste. Dredge the veal in flour; coat with wash of eggs and milk, well beaten together; and then coat with bread crumbs. Heat the oil and fry the schnitzel until golden brown on both sides. Drain meat.

The Holstein garnish is a fried egg and anchovy fillets and capers on top of the schnitzel. You may add a paprika cream sauce (see recipe below). Serves 6.

SALEM TAVERN'S PAPRIKA CREAM SAUCE

2 tablespoons butter
2 tablespoons all-purpose
　flour
2 cups half-and-half

1 tablespoon white wine
1 heaping tablespoon
　Hungarian paprika
salt and pepper

Melt butter in saucepan and add flour. Stir until all butter is absorbed. Add half-and-half, stirring briskly to avoid lumps. Simmer until thickened, then add wine and paprika. Season to taste. Yields 2 cups.

SALEM TAVERN'S CORNY CORN BREAD

2 eggs
1 cup sour cream
1 small can creamed corn

1 cup Ballard corn bread
　mix
½ cup corn oil

Beat eggs in a bowl. Add remaining ingredients. Mix well and pour into greased 8- by 8-inch pan. Bake at 350 degrees for 45 minutes. Serves 9.

ZEVELY HOUSE
Winston-Salem

ZEVELY HOUSE

You get the feeling that Van Neman Zevely, the cabinetmaker who built Zevely House in 1815, and its current owner, Pete Smitherman, were cut from the same cloth. It seems that Zevely defied Moravian custom by refusing to ask the church elders for permission to marry his fiancée, Johanna Shober. Later this faux pas was corrected, but not, one would imagine, soon enough to satisfy the ostracized Miss Shober. Therefore, Pete says chuckling, "When we built the other restaurant next door, it seemed only right to call it Johanna Shober's."

As you listen to Smitherman describe the agony and frustration of moving the wonderful old Flemish brick house to the downtown's fashionable West End, where it stands as the oldest structure in Winston township, you recognize his special feelings for sturdy architecture. "It had to be saved," he said. And saved it was, through months of meticulous restoration.

Now you may dine in a blue and white, antique-filled setting. Zevely was not a pretentious man, nor is Pete, who prefers to preserve a casual atmosphere with a menu as unintimidating in price as it is in choice. You can order anything from a good hamburger, with an accent on good, to Veal Cordon Bleu.

For lunch I like the beer-battered fresh vegetables followed by a bowl of French onion soup, and all topped off with the famous pumpkin muffins. The muffins have become such a trademark that Pete had one enshrined in plastic at the bar.

At dinner I rack my brain trying to choose, because it's all fantastic! Veal Oscar, with crabmeat and asparagus, is "Wunderbar," but so is the stuffed breast of chicken in puff pastry. My husband, a steak man, is pleased with the six different cuts and preparations of steak. Dieters can feast on a lemon-broiled Carolina mountain rainbow trout or scallops with artichokes—minus the au gratin.

If I'm allowed dessert I'll choose the super apple-walnut

pie, and someday I'm going to find the courage to sample the Turtle Pie.

You'll discover an enticing selection of mixed drinks, or you may choose one of the fine wines or beers to complement your meal.

Zevely House is located at 901 West Fourth Street in Winston-Salem. Lunch is served from 11:30 a.m. to 2:00 p.m., and dinner from 6:00 to 9:00 p.m., Tuesday through Sunday. For reservations call (919) 725–6666.

ZEVELY HOUSE'S FRENCH ONION SOUP

5 medium onions	¼ stick of butter
3 quarts beef stock	dash of white wine
(see Index)	10 slices Swiss cheese
2 cups croutons	

Slice onions thin. Place in a large pot and cover with beef stock. Cook on medium high for about an hour. Add salt and pepper, wine, and butter. Pour into individual ovenproof soup bowls and top with a slice of Swiss cheese and croutons; place under broiler until cheese melts. Serves 10.

ZEVELY HOUSE'S VEAL OSCAR

4 6-ounce veal cutlets	¼ cup white wine
8 ounces king crabmeat	16 spears fresh asparagus
½ cup flour	Béarnaise sauce (see Index)
2 to 3 tablespoons butter	1 cup grated Swiss cheese

Pound veal thin. Lightly dredge veal in flour, then sauté in butter over high heat for 3 to 4 minutes on each side. Remove meat and deglaze pan with wine. Wrap veal around asparagus, place in casserole dish, seam-side down, and top with crabmeat. Ladle a tablespoon of Béarnaise sauce over each cutlet and smother with grated Swiss cheese. Broil until cheese is melted. Serves 4.

ZEVELY HOUSE'S PUMPKIN MUFFINS

1 cup or more canned
  pumpkin
2 eggs
⅓ cup water
⅓ cup butter, melted
1⅔ cups sifted flour
1½ cups sugar
⅓ cup raisins

1 teaspoon baking soda
1 teaspoon pumpkin pie
  spice
¼ teaspoon salt
¼ teaspoon baking powder
⅛ teaspoon ground cloves
18 paper muffin liners
Pam

Mix wet ingredients thoroughly; add dry ingredients, and stir until blended. Spray paper liners with Pam and fill them ⅔ full. Bake at 350 degrees until golden brown, about 35 minutes. Yields 18.

ZEVELY HOUSE'S CHICKEN IN PUFF PASTRY CORDON BLEU

4 chicken breasts,
  skinned and deboned
salt and pepper
1⅓ cups grated
  Swiss cheese

4 thin slices of ham
4 5- by 6-inch sheets puff
  pastry (Pepperidge Farm)
1 egg white
Béarnaise sauce (see Index)

Flatten chicken breasts with meat mallet. Add salt and pepper to taste. Place a slice of cheese and a slice of ham on top of each chicken breast. Place chicken in center of pastry; wrap pastry around chicken, and fold like an envelope, squeezing seams tightly together. Seal seam with whipped egg white and brush egg white along seam. Bake at 400 degrees for approximately 25 to 30 minutes until the pastry is golden brown.

Cover with Béarnaise sauce and serve. Serves 4.

LA CHAUDIÈRE
Winston-Salem

LA CHAUDIÈRE

Trrue Gallic charm greets you the moment you step upon the terra-cotta tiled floor of La Chaudière. Now, who but the innovative French would think of converting a furnace room into one of North Carolina's most superb restaurants? The Jones and Monteran families did. This enterprising ensemble converted a group of rooms that heated, through a maze of underground tunnels, the vast R. J. Reynolds estate. In fact, the room that currently is the wine cellar served as the original entrance to the underground passageway, which was built in 1917.

Is there a dungeonlike feeling? No, indeed. The antique windows, French doors, and profusion of red geraniums produce a light and airy country French atmosphere. Even foot-thick plaster walls are amusingly adorned with antique prints, tapestry reproductions, and fine watercolors from the Monteran family's collection.

The first time I dined at La Chaudière I ordered the rack of lamb grilled with herbs, Escargots de Bourgogne and a salad. Voila! My dinner companions raved about an appetizer of shrimp in puff pastry and Saga cheese, which they claim has addicted them.

The artistic pastry chef, Charles DeVries, can even make the puff pastry encasing crabmeat resemble a baby crab. I discovered why my pastries don't taste like his. He works in a pastry room kept at an even sixty degrees. My two favorite desserts are Boite aux Chocolat, which is rum-soaked cake and butter cream covered in chocolate, and a layered praline meringue called Sucées. It certainly was a success.

I was told that mixed drinks are not served because, in the traditional French manner, wines are served to tease your taste buds and prepare you for simple but classic cooking. Therefore, I chose a delicious Château de Tigne rosé.

The chefs, Didier Monteran and Ted Herman, recommended the Poulet au Riesling, adding that you must never cook with a wine that you wouldn't serve at your table. For dieters, they suggested the Terrine de Legumes with a vinaigrette sauce, and said they would "decalorize" any dish for you if given sufficient notice.

My appreciation goes to the restaurant's owners, Thad and Catherine Jones, for providing an elegant yet casual approach to dining with the charmingly different French sense of humor.

La Chaudière is located at 120 Reynolda Road in Winston-Salem. Lunch is served from 11:30 a.m. to 2:30 p.m., and dinner from 6:30 to 9:30 p.m., Tuesday through Saturday. Sunday brunch is from 11:30 a.m. to 2:30 p.m. For reservations call (919) 748–0269.

LA CHAUDIÈRE'S
FILLET OF PINK SNAPPER IN PASTRY

4 deboned fillets of pink
   snapper (may also be
   called silver)
salt
cayenne pepper
½ cup white wine

½ cup fish fumet
   (see Index)
2 sheets puff pastry
   (Pepperidge Farm)
1 egg white
½ cup capers
fresh parsley sprigs

Cut pastry sheets in half and roll out to about ⅛-inch thick. Place each fillet of snapper in center of each pastry and sprinkle with salt and cayenne. Then wrap: Fold half of the bottom over snapper; now fold half the top over snapper; fold one end square over snapper as you would fold an envelope. On the opposite end, fold the corners at an angle so that the end comes to a point. Seal the seams with egg white. Wrap each snapper in plastic wrap and refrigerate for at least 10 minutes.

Remove pastry from refrigerator and decorate unseamed side: Pinch square end for tail. With a knife, draw deep lines into tail. Now draw a deep arc for face. With round bottle top or any kitchen accessory, cut a deep eye. With the side of a spoon, press the scale effect on side of fish and make appropriate slit for mouth. Rewrap in plastic wrap and return to refrigerator for later baking. (This is one of those nice make-ahead dishes.)

Preheat oven to 400 degrees. Insert fish, then reduce heat to 375 degrees. Cook for 20 to 25 minutes, until golden.

In a saucepan, heat fish fumet and wine until reduced to half. Place in blender with capers, salt, and cayenne; blend.

Place on plate with baked snapper. Garnish with parsley. Serves 4.

LA CHAUDIÈRE'S POULET AU BASILIC
(Chicken with Basil Sauce)

4 chicken breasts	12 cherry tomatoes
¾ cup unwhipped cream	salt and pepper
¼ cup sour cream	2 tablespoons butter
2 tablespoons finely	¼ cup white wine
chopped fresh basil	toothpicks

Combine cream and sour cream, and let stand at room temperature of 65 degrees for 24 hours. (This is creme fraiche.)

Debone and skin chicken breasts and pound them thin. Place ¾ teaspoon basil in center of flattened meat, add three cherry tomatoes and salt and pepper. Then roll up chicken and secure with toothpicks. Sauté in butter, cooking side with seal first. Then cook on both sides until done. Remove chicken and deglaze pan with wine. Stir in creme fraiche, and cook until liquid is reduced to half. Then add 1 table-spoon chopped fresh basil. This gives a lovely green color. Pour over chicken and serve immediately. Serves 4.

SALEM COTTON CO.
Winston-Salem

SALEM COTTON CO. I suppose you can enter Salem Cotton Co. through the front door on Brookstown Avenue. However, on my first visit I happened to go in through the back second-floor entrance and was so visually stunned that it has become my preferred approach when I want to dazzle my first-time guests.

The open two-story interior, endowed with modernized nineteenth-century atmosphere, is a show-stopping view. From the balcony you overlook the main dining room, whose dominating feature is a massive 1837 black steam boiler that once provided the energy for the manufacture of yarn for the Confederate soldiers' uniforms. Just opposite the boiler room is a beautiful glass-enclosed room that leads onto a garden patio. If you are dining on the patio, you may see someone gathering the herbs that will give your meal its distinctive flavor.

Part of the excitement of dining at Salem Cotton Co. is that you never know what will be happening there. I once took a friend to lunch for her birthday and wandered upon a fashion show featuring hand-woven garments. Then, when our waiter realized that a birthday was being celebrated, we received complimentary glasses of champagne and Godiva chocolates.

For lunch I endorse the Pocket Pita Sandwich, which is stuffed with sautéed flank steak, olives, and sprouts, and is garnished with pepper slaw. But when dieting, I go with the Fisherman's Caesar Salad, which features tuna and smoked oysters. For dessert I waver between the lemon soufflé and the Kahlua parfait. If in the mood, I find an elegant treat to conclude any meal is the coffee with Grand Marnier. The wine list, as you might expect, leaves little to be desired.

The restaurant's exquisite bonus is being able to enjoy your dinner to the rapturous tones of the harpist. Salem Cotton Co. is truly an unusual escape from the humdrum, as are the shops and art galleries that occupy the other half of the Brookstown Mill complex.

Salem Cotton Co. is located at 200 Brookstown Avenue in Winston-Salem. Lunch is served from 11:30 a. m. to 2:30 p. m. Monday through Saturday, and dinner from 5:30 to 10:00 p. m. seven days a week. For reservations call (919) 723–9475.

SALEM COTTON CO.'S
DUCK STROGANOFF

1 4½- to 5-pound duck	1 tablespoon minced
1 tablespoon butter	parsley
1 shallot, chopped	salt and pepper
1 cup sliced mushrooms	monosodium glutamate
½ cup sherry	1 cup beef stock
1 teaspoon paprika	(see Index)
juice of one lemon	½ cup sour cream

Bake duck in a moderate oven for 30 to 35 minutes per pound, or for 40 minutes in a microwave.

Melt butter in a saucepan; sauté shallot until transparent. Add mushrooms and sherry, and stir for 10 minutes. Add seasonings and stir in beef stock; simmer for 10 minutes. Stir in sour cream, making sure that it does not separate; simmer for 10 more minutes. Slice duck into 1-inch chunks. Carefully fold duck into sauce, and continue simmering for another 5 minutes.

Garnish with more chopped parsley. Serve with wild rice, nutted brown rice, or over noodles and spaetzle. Serves 4.

SALEM COTTON CO.'S LEMON SOUFFLÉ

1 cup confectioners' sugar	grated peel of 1 lemon
5 eggs	2 ounces apricot-flavored
juice of 2 lemons	brandy

Sieve the sugar. Separate the eggs and beat the whites until stiff. Add the lemon peel and juice to the egg yolks, stir in the sugar, and whip until creamy. Fold in the egg whites and brandy. Put in a 1-quart buttered soufflé dish and bake at 375 degrees for 20 minutes.

Serve at once. Serves 4 to 6.

SALEM COTTON CO.'S NOODLE PUDDING

1 pound broad noodles
⅛ cup sliced almonds
2 eggs
2 tablespoons vanilla
3 apples, peeled and
  cut fine

⅜ cup white raisins
1 cup milk
nutmeg
cinnamon
butter

Cook noodles according to package directions. Drain and mix with remaining ingredients. Turn into ovenproof dish and bake at 300 degrees for 35 minutes. Serves 4 to 6.

TANGLEWOOD MANOR HOUSE
Clemmons

TANGLEWOOD MANOR HOUSE

The doors at Tanglewood Manor House won't stay locked. "It's because Mr. Will wouldn't put up with a door locked in his house," explained an employee. "And after nightfall, when the lights flicker and go out in the room where he played poker, that's just Mr. Will's prankish way of telling people it's time to go to bed."

Employees of the late Will Reynolds believe that his spirit continues to oversee his 1859 home in Tanglewood Park. That handsome two-story white brick house, now a restaurant with lodging facilities, also retains its original spirit through the country chintz decor. It was this casual atmosphere that Kate and Will Reynolds sought to preserve when they bought and made additions to the house and grounds in the late twenties. Loving the recreation that the lake and woods offered, the Reynoldses built stables and a racetrack, which were used in the training of Reynolds' harness racers. The success of the horses is evidenced by the many trophies remaining on display in the Manor House.

Initially, a sylvan peacefulness draws me to the restaurant, but it is more than tranquility that I find. I feel as if I've come to dinner at a friend's home. As in the days of the Reynoldses, flowers from the rose garden grace every room of the house. Even the food, which is a blend of continental cuisine with Southern overtones, makes me think my host has gone to special pains simply to please me. And the restaurant's staff does go to extra pains. Whether working with the diet of a calorie watcher or of someone with health problems, the staff adapts individual needs to the Manor's five-course menu.

The wine list, offering a range of domestic and imported vintages, has been selected to coordinate with the Manor's choice of three entrées. I particularly like the marinated shrimp appetizer, followed by either Chicken Cordon Bleu or prime rib. For dessert I am torn between chocolate mousse or Black Bottom Pie if they are on the menu. The mousse invariably wins.

In my opinion, dining at the Manor House is the perfect

finale to a day at Tanglewood. Arrive early, then spend the day horseback riding, fishing, swimming, canoeing, or walking through gardens that appear to be a fairy tale come true.

Tanglewood Manor House Restaurant is located in Tanglewood Park at Clemmons, about 10 miles west of Winston-Salem off I-40. Dinner is served from 6:00 to 10:00 p. m. Tuesday through Saturday. For reservations call (919) 766–7367.

TANGLEWOOD MANOR HOUSE RESTAURANT'S MARINATED SHRIMP PORT GIBSON

2½ pounds medium shrimp
½ cup salad oil
¼ cup vinegar
¾ cup minced celery
1¼ tablespoons grated
  onions
½ clove garlic, minced

2½ tablespoons minced
  parsley
2½ tablespoons horseradish
2½ tablespoons Dijon
  mustard
¾ teaspoon salt
⅛ teaspoon pepper

2 tablespoons paprika

Bring a large pot of lightly salted water to a boil; add shrimp. When water comes to a boil again, remove from heat and drain shrimp immediately. Ice down shrimp until cool. Mix all other ingredients and coat shrimp. Marinate overnight. Serves 10 to 12.

TANGLEWOOD MANOR HOUSE RESTAURANT'S RED SNAPPER BOURSIN

4 6-ounce snapper fillets
2 tablespoons clarified
  butter

3 to 4 shallots, chopped
¼ cup dry vermouth

Boursin sauce:
½ cup Boursin cheese,
  softened
4 egg yolks

½ cup heavy whipping
  cream

For the sauce, whip cheese and egg yolks together and set aside. Whip cream and fold into cheese mixture; mix thoroughly. Refrigerate.

Sweat the shallots in skillet of hot clarified butter. Remove shallots; add fillets and cook on one side. Return shallots to pan and cook fillets on remaining side. Remove from pan and place in broiler pan.

Deglaze skillet with vermouth and pour over fillets. Coat fillets with Boursin sauce and broil until golden.

May also use deboned chicken that has been pounded thin. Serves 4.

TANGLEWOOD MANOR HOUSE RESTAURANT'S TAR HEEL PIE

12 ounces cream cheese, softened
½ cup sugar
½ pint whipping cream

1½ medium bananas, sliced
1 9-inch deep-dish pie shell, baked

Blueberry glaze:
1 package frozen blueberries

⅓ cup sugar
1 tablespoon cornstarch

Mix softened cream cheese with sugar. Whip cream until stiff peaks form. Carefully fold cream into cheese mixture and mix until thoroughly blended. Slice bananas and place in bottom and sides of pie shell. Pour cheese mixture over bananas and chill until firm.

Combine ingredients for glaze and cook over low heat until thick. Be careful not to break up the berries. Cool to room temperature.

Spoon glaze evenly over cheese mixture and chill several hours or overnight.

THE POLLIROSA
Tobaccoville

THE POLLIROSA

Back when The Pollirosa restaurant's two-story log structure was used as a residence, a community dutch oven was attached to one side of it. Women of the area would gather there and bake up to fifty pies at a time, and as the women cooked, the men would fiddle.

The Hauser family brought the Moravian tradition of "making music when breaking bread" from Germany when they immigrated to Pennsylvania in 1757. Eight generations later, Millie and Johnny Rierson revived that tradition when, in 1965, they opened the Pollirosa, a restaurant that serves old-fashioned food and old-time music.

The restaurant is named for two of the family's best cooks: Polly Shamel, who lived in the log plantation house during the Civil War, and Rosa Rierson, who became its resident during the days of the community oven. The tradition of their cooking lives on in The Pollirosa's menu, which features such dishes as chicken and dumplings, fresh home-grown vegetables, and the best pound cake you've ever put in your mouth.

The popularity of The Pollirosa can be proven by the fact that it keeps expanding. At first, music and food were offered only every other Saturday night, but now the restaurant is open from Wednesday through Sunday every week. New dining rooms were added, and eventually a large room was built as a music hall. Two gospel groups currently alternate there with the Rierson family's Country and Western band.

Music and food are equally pleasurable, and both are offered for one incredibly low price. You can even get as many "seconds" as your diet can afford. When I asked Mrs. Rierson how she and her husband could offer so much for so little, she just smiled and said, "Cooperation—between us, the good Lord, and the good earth."

The Pollirosa restaurant is located on Hollyberry Lane off Spainhour Mill Road in Tobaccoville, which is 15 miles north of Winston-Salem on U. S. 52. Dinner is served from 5:00 to

9:00 p. m. Wednesday through Saturday, and from noon to 8:00 p. m. Sunday. For reservations call (919) 983–5352.

THE POLLIROSA'S CUCUMBER PICKLES

1 quart vinegar
2 quarts water
3 gallons cucumbers

1 teaspoon canning salt
  per jar
6 teaspoons sugar per jar

In large pot, place water and vinegar. Bring to a boil and add fresh, clean cucumbers, whole or sliced. Cucumbers should remain only long enough to change to an olive-green color, but should not boil. Pack cucumbers in sterilized glass quart jars and add one teaspoon salt and six teaspoons sugar to each jar. Fill each jar with vinegar water to ½ inch from top. Seal jars. Yields about 12 quarts.

THE POLLIROSA'S BEST POUND CAKE

3 cups sugar
1 stick margarine
1 cup shortening
6 eggs
½ teaspoon vanilla extract

½ teaspoon lemon extract
pinch of salt
3½ cups sifted plain
  or cake flour

Cream sugar, margarine, and shortening. Beat eggs and add to mixture; add vanilla, lemon, and salt. Slowly add flour, mixing thoroughly. Pour batter in a greased bundt or pound cake pan. Bake at 300 degrees for 45 minutes, then raise the temperature to 325 degrees and bake for another 45 minutes.

THE POLLIROSA'S GRAHAM CRACKER CAKE

½ pound butter
2 cups sugar
5 eggs
2 teaspoons baking powder
1 pound box graham
  crackers, crushed

1 cup milk
1 cup flake coconut
1 large can pineapple,
  drained

Cream butter and sugar; add eggs, one at a time, and mix well. In a separate bowl, add baking powder to graham cracker crumbs. Stir into moist ingredients. Add milk and coconut, mixing well. Pour into 3 greased and floured cake pans. Bake at 350 degrees for 25 to 30 minutes. Remove from oven and cool.

Place one layer of cake on a plate and spread with ⅓ of crushed pineapple; repeat procedure with remaining layers and add icing (see recipe below).

THE POLLIROSA'S ICING
FOR GRAHAM CRACKER CAKE

1 stick butter   **1 box confectioners' sugar**
1 egg   **1 teaspoon vanilla**

Soften butter, beat egg, and mix at low speed. Add vanilla and fold in confectioners' sugar.

Ice cooled cake.

KATHRYN'S
Lexington

KATHRYN'S

When I approached Kathryn's restaurant, I was hoping to be greeted by the ghost who is said to reside in Colonel Maybry's 1830 home. No such luck. I had heard that the spirit of "Aunt Sally," who was officially included in the house's deed, seems to remain upstairs. Many items are unexplainably rearranged up there, and doors are heard to open and shut. Unfortunately, she made neither an appearance nor a noise as I toured the four upstairs dining rooms, each of which is named for one of the former owners of the house.

Back downstairs, in the dining room that is thought to have served as Lexington's post office when Colonel Maybry was postmaster, the tinkling tones from a player piano gave me pause for thought until I remembered it really was a player piano! How amenable one is to suggestion.

My luncheon in the attractive room, with its original wood floors and tiled fireplace, was almost more than I could eat, and I only ordered half a sandwich and soup. Since Reubens are a favorite, I was particularly pleased with the one at Kathryn's; the homemade bread made it extra tasty. The homemade asparagus soup was a new treat that I hope to repeat soon. For dessert I had a creamy Key-lime pie with an herb tea that I chose from the adjoining room's delicatessen. Had I wanted to diet I could have had a tossed salad for lunch and broiled flounder or steak for dinner. A most unusual collection of wines includes Magnolia, which is made at North Carolina's Duplin Winery. Only one bottle was left. Guess who bought it?

Kathryn's is part of Oak Grove Restorations, so plan to meander back in time through the restored historical structures that are now gift shops.

Kathryn's is located at 308 East Center Street in Lexington. Meals are served from 7:00 a. m. to 9:00 p. m. Monday through Thursday, and to 10:00 p. m. Friday and Saturday. For reservations call (704) 243–2533.

KATHRYN'S ARTICHOKE DIP

1 small can artichoke
  hearts
1¼ cups mayonnaise

1 cup grated Parmesan
  cheese
pinch of garlic powder

Dice artichoke hearts fine. Mix mayonnaise, cheese, and garlic until smooth. Add artichoke hearts.

May be served hot or cold. Yields over 2 cups.

KATHRYN'S BAKED BRIE

1 small ring Brie
1 tablespoon butter

1 tablespoon slivered
  almonds

Put almonds on top of Brie; place butter over almonds. Bake at 350 degrees for about 10 minutes, or until crust rises. Peel away crust and serve. Serves 4 to 6.

KATHRYN'S GRINDER SANDWICH

⅛ pound roast beef,
  sliced thin
French roll
mayonnaise or
  salad dressing
¼ green pepper, chopped

¼ onion, chopped
1 slice Provolone cheese
½ cup au jus dip (found in
  gourmet section of
  food store)

Spread bread with dressing of choice, then add peppers, onions, roast beef, and cheese.

Serve au jus dip on the side. Serves 1.

KATHRYN'S ONION CASSEROLE

1 stick butter
1½ cups crushed buttery
   crackers

5 large onions
1 cup Parmesan cheese

Melt 6 tablespoons butter and pour over crushed crackers; set aside to cool. Slice onions into very thin rings and sauté in 2 tablespoons butter until transparent. Pour half of the onions into a 1½-quart greased casserole. Cover with half the Parmesan cheese and half the crushed crackers. Repeat procedure and bake, uncovered, at 325 degrees for about 30 minutes, or until golden brown. Serves 8.

KATHRYN'S CALABASH SHRIMP

1 pound medium shrimp,
   cleaned and deveined
1 cup cornmeal

1 tablespoon seafood
   seasoning
2 eggs, beaten
oil for deep frying

Mix cornmeal and seafood seasoning. Wash shrimp in egg, then dip in cornmeal and seafood seasoning mixture. Deep fry 2 to 3 minutes, or until golden brown.

Serve with onion casserole. Serves 3 to 4.

O'NEILL'S
Charlotte

O'NEILL'S

Unfortunately, not every day can invoke festivity at O'Neill's on quite the scale on which it occurs on Saint Patrick's Day. On this occasion, Mike and Pat O'Neill rope off the street in front of their restaurant. Jazz and Dixieland bands play, and senior citizens delight the crowds by jigging to the Charlotte Bagpipers. Aye, 'tis a merry time to be sure, especially when keg upon keg of free green beer is drunk to wash down the Irish stew. As O'Neill recalled, "Last year about 3,990 of the 4,000 celebrants had a wee bit too much of the spirits."

One of the pub's most popular drinks is called the Red Hand of Ireland. It is named in honor of one of O'Neill's lusty ancestors, who is said to have won Ireland in a sea race. It seems that when he saw he was losing, he whipped out his sword, severed his hand, and tossed it to shore in order to be the first to touch the sacred sod.

Ah yes, the Irish can spin them, can't they? It doesn't have to be Saint Paddy's day for the blarney to blow; you can enjoy O'Neill's jovial atmosphere at lunch, dinner, or happy hour, any day but Sunday.

O'Neill's is located in a building that began as E. Reed Russell's handkerchief factory back in 1906. That enterprise was successful until 1936, when modern technology introduced the disposable Kleenex. The building knew many occupants during the next forty-odd years, until the revitalization of downtown Charlotte spurred the O'Neills to renovate the convenient location. The walls were stripped to expose the natural brick, and the heart-pine floor and tables were recycled from an old cotton mill. An oak bar came out of Charlotte's Greystone Manor, and the back bar was originally part of the sacristy of an old Baptist church.

Although the authentic Irish dishes, salads, and meal-sized sandwiches have made the working force regulars at O'Neill's for lunch, I would kick off my high heels, change into jeans, and be the first one at the happy hour. You won't find a happier or more sporting place around. Every thirty minutes a large wheel of fortune is spun to set the price of drinks for that period. This can be a good deal, especially if the marker lands on half-price. Another tempting feature is the free hot appetizers.

The relaxed mood will blend right into dinner. That menu offers corned beef and cabbage, Irish stew, and my two favorites; Regina's Chicken and the specialty, roast beef on a hoagie bun. If you are not up to all that, you can do a calorie count-down with a steak or vegetable salad.

Thursday through Saturday you will find musical entertainment from Irish ballads to folk-rock. The Irish know best how to exercise the verb "enjoy," so don't be shy. Invest yourself in some true Irish culture, and you're bound to become a convert.

O'Neill's is located at 118 West Fifth Street in Charlotte. Lunch is served from 11:30 a.m. to 2:30 p.m., and dinner from 5:00 to 11:00 p.m., Monday through Saturday. Happy hour is 4:30 to 7:00 p.m. Reservations are not necessary, but the number is (704) 333–7845.

O'NEILL'S RED HAND OF IRELAND

⅓ cup cranberry juice   ½ cup orange juice
1¼ ounces vodka   Cheerwine

Combine juices and vodka in an 8-ounce glass. Fill with ice and Cheerwine. Serves 1.

O'NEILL'S IRISH STEW

1½ pounds leg of lamb   salt and pepper
1 pound potatoes   ¼ teaspoon dried parsley
1½ yellow onions

Cut fat from lamb and cut lamb into bite-sized chunks. Peel potatoes and slice ¼-inch thick. Peel onions and slice ¼-inch thick. In a heavy, long, flat casserole, layer onions, potatoes, and lamb, ending with onions. Sprinkle salt and pepper lib-

119

erally over each layer of potatoes. Add enough water to cover top layer with about an inch. Bring to a boil on top of stove, then cover and bake at 325 degrees until potatoes are soft. Cool and refrigerate overnight.

Skim any accumulated fat from surface, sprinkle with parsley, and heat through. Serves 4 to 6.

O'NEILL'S CHICKEN REGINA

6 chicken breasts, deboned
2 cups uncooked rice
2 large stalks broccoli
1 can cream of mushroom
  soup
1 can cream of chicken soup

½ cup sour cream
1 tablespoon lemon juice
1 tablespoon sherry
1 tablespoon curry
½ cup grated sharp cheddar
  cheese

Cook rice. Cook chicken in boiling water until done. Cut up broccoli and cook in salted water until crunchy. In a greased casserole, layer rice, chicken, and broccoli. Combine soups, sour cream, lemon juice, sherry, and curry. Blend until thoroughly mixed and pour over chicken combination. Spread grated cheese evenly on top, and cook at 325 degrees for 25 minutes. Serves 6 to 8.

O'NEILL'S VEGETABLE MUNCH

1 bunch broccoli, chopped
1 head cauliflower, chopped
6 carrots, sliced thin
3 celery stalks, sliced thin
10 spring onions, diced
2 cucumbers, peeled and
  chopped
1 cup vegetable oil

¾ cup clear cider vinegar
1 tablespoon white sugar
1 tablespoon dill weed
1 tablespoon monosodium
  glutamate
1 teaspoon salt
1 teaspoon pepper
1 teaspoon garlic salt

After chopping and dicing vegetables to desired sizes, place them together in a bowl. Combine seasonings, oil, vinegar, and sugar, and pour over vegetables. Cover and marinate in refrigerator until cold. Serves 8 to 12.

THE LAMP LIGHTER
Charlotte

THE LAMP LIGHTER   A Mediterranean-style house built in 1925 by the Van Ness family has been redecorated to a grandness that would please the flamboyant taste of Mrs. Van Ness. We owe a debt of appreciation to this lady for her reverence for high-quality birch paneling and Doric columns, which remain a part of the interior. The present owners of the house, Charles and Marian Tucker, have taken special care to preserve its intimacy. The warm chocolate-brown decor is set off by creatively positioned chandeliers that subtly blink to the passersby. The Tuckers' wonderful collection of European paintings look as if they have always been part of this setting, yet they have been in the family's two previous restaurants in England.

Before dinner at the Lamp Lighter, we enjoyed wine at the bar. It is just beyond a marble fireplace that operates year-round, with the aid of an air-conditioning vent in the summer. The wine list is a creative blend of domestic and imported choices, and the restaurant also features a selection of over seventy-five liqueurs.

The menu is varied but leans toward continental cuisine. The herring is an outstanding appetizer, but I've never been known to pass up escargot. Prepared with garlic butter and parsley, it was a true bud teaser. For my main course, I chose scallops with rice pilaf. The escargots were complemented, if not excelled, by the delicious fresh scallops. To accompany our meal, a lovely dry Vouvray by Alexis Lichine was perfect. Being Irish, I felt compelled to order the Irish Coffee Cream Pie, which I enjoyed; but a taste of Marian Tucker's caramelized custard cream with almonds was the pièce de résistance. Then my delicious meal culminated with Lamp Lighter Coffee, which owes a romantic kinship to Irish Coffee.

No, I didn't diet, but I could have ordered any number of broiled fish, chicken, or steak entrées, had I felt the need to do so.

An important charm of this restaurant is its ability to slow down the clock and allow its guests to dine in an unhurried atmosphere. After the liqueur was served, I was astounded to discover that I had been inside this lovely restaurant for over four hours. The relaxed soft glow that The Lamp Lighter imparts somehow seeps into your being and makes time seem to fall away.

The Lamp Lighter is located at 1065 East Morehead Street in Charlotte. Dinner is served from 6:00 to 10:00 p. m. Monday through Saturday. For reservations call (704) 372–5343.

THE LAMP LIGHTER'S CHICKEN PECAN

2 large chicken breasts, deboned and cut in half	3 tablespoons Dijon mustard
salt and pepper	⅔ cup ground pecans
10 tablespoons butter	6 tablespoons vegetable oil
⅔ cup sour cream	

Place chicken between two pieces of waxed paper and lightly flatten with a meat mallet. Season with salt and pepper. Melt 6 tablespoons butter in a small pan; remove from heat and whisk in 2 tablespoons mustard. Dip each piece of chicken into mustard mixture and coat heavily with ground pecans. Melt 4 tablespoons butter in a skillet; stir in the oil. When blended and hot, sauté chicken about 4 minutes on each side, or until chicken is cooked. Remove from skillet and keep warm.

Deglaze the skillet with sour cream and whisk the remaining mustard into the sauce. Sauce should retain a strong mustardy flavor. Remove from heat.

Present by placing a dollop of the sauce in the middle of a warmed dinner plate and covering dollop with the chicken. Only a small portion of sauce should accompany each piece, in order not to overpower the chicken. Serves 3 to 4.

THE LAMP LIGHTER'S TARTUFI

1 cup superfine sugar
⅔ cup Dutch process cocoa
2 teaspoons instant
  espresso powder
⅓ cup water
4 egg yolks
10 Maraschino cherries

2 tablespoons rum
1 cup whipping cream
⅓ cup chopped toasted
  almonds
shaved chocolate for
  garnish

Stem and pit cherries; rinse them, then soak in rum.

Sift sugar, cocoa, and espresso into a heavy to medium saucepan. Whisk in the water. Place over medium heat and bring to a boil, stirring constantly until all sugar is dissolved and mixture is smooth, about 10 minutes. In a large bowl, beat egg yolks with electric mixer on high speed. When yolks are light and fluffy, reduce to medium speed and add hot chocolate mixture in a slow, steady stream. Continue to beat until cool. Chill one hour.

Remove cherries from rum with slotted spoon and set aside. Mix rum into cooled chocolate. Whip cream until stiff peaks form. Stir one large spoonful into chocolate mixture to loosen, blending well. Gently fold in remaining whipped cream and chopped almonds, being careful not to deflate whipped cream. Fill ten individual serving cups less than half full with chocolate mixture. Place a cherry in the center; fill to within half an inch of the top. Sprinkle shaved chocolate lightly on top. Cover with plastic and then with foil. Freeze a minimum of four hours.

Thaw 5 to 10 minutes before serving. Will keep for a month. Serves 10.

SPOON'S
Charlotte

SPOON'S

When people come into an ice cream parlor they are happy, because ice cream is a treat!" Spoon's current manager said. It is an affordable treat, reckoned Whitney Spoon, who began making his ice cream in 1929, at the beginning of the Depression. In the early days, Mr. Spoon filled a leather bag with dry ice and ice cream, strapped it to a man's back, and sent him out on the street or to ball games to hawk his wares. The popularity of his high-quality ice cream soon allowed Spoon to open his own ice cream parlor.

Today, there are new yellow-and-white checked curtains in the window, but that is the only change that has been made at Spoon's Ice Cream Company since the late twenties. You'll see the same marble counter, sculptured tin ceiling, old tile floor, and wooden tables that have always been here. When Mrs. Spoon took over the operation, she wanted to remodel and make it look "cute," but she soon found that people didn't want "cute." They wanted the same old-timey unair-conditioned place where children could ride their bikes through the front door. You see, adults and children come to Spoon's for the thirty-eight varieties of ice cream and sherbet, not for the fancy decor. They like it so much that they wait in line on Sunday.

I've been visiting Spoon's for over eighteen years, and I have always chosen the double cone because I can get four different scoops of ice cream on it. During my recent visit, I was introduced to a new luncheon and dinner inspiration called Sub on a Spud. This is a baked potato filled with sour cream and layers of roast beef, ham, and corned beef interlaced with different cheeses, then topped with chopped onion, bacon bits, and more butter. It was so sensational and I ate so much that I only had room to sample about ten flavors of ice cream.

A taste of each flavor is given on one of those old-fashioned flat wooden spoons. Coconut used to be my favorite, but I have to admit that the new strawberry cheesecake beats the competition, with butterscotch chip as the runner-up. My favorite sherbet is the tangerine, but I am also leaning hard toward the raspberry.

I was surprised to learn that adults eat eighty percent of the ice cream at Spoon's. What is the favorite flavor? If you said vanilla, you were right.

As children roller-skated past our table, I asked what dieters could eat, and the reply was, "Are you kidding, we don't even carry Sweet'n Low." At Spoon's that's just the way it is—the way it was.

Spoon's is located at Seventh Street and Hawthorne Lane in Charlotte. It is open daily from 10:00 a.m. to 11:00 p.m. Reservations are not necessary, but the telephone number is (704) 376–0974.

SPOON'S SUB ON A SPUD

4 12-ounce baked potatoes
  in foil
8 tablespoons butter
8 tablespoons sour cream
8 slices corned beef
4 slices Swiss cheese
8 slices ham
4 slices American cheese
8 slices roast beef
4 slices mozzarella cheese
½ cup finely diced onion
8 slices bacon, fried and
  crumbled

Flatten the baked potato by hitting it hard with the palm of your hand. Cut down center to 1 inch from each end, and squeeze potato out of cut.

Work 1 tablespoon butter and 1 tablespoon sour cream down to bottom of potato as you make a hole in the middle. Layer with 2 slices corned beef and 1 slice Swiss cheese; 2 slices ham and 1 slice American cheese; 2 slices roast beef and 1 slice mozzarella. Add more butter and sour cream, and top each potato with onion and bacon. Put under broiler at 425 degrees until cheese melts. Serves 4.

SPOON'S STRAWBERRY CHEESECAKE ICE CREAM

1 quart buttermilk
2 cups heavy whipping
  cream
1½ cups sugar

2 tablespoons vanilla
  extract
1 jar strawberry topping

Blend first four ingredients thoroughly. Put in freezer unit of refrigerator. Stir well after it begins to freeze and return again to freezer. You can put remixed ingredients in an ice cream maker and use according to machine's directions.

Serve with strawberry topping. Yields 1½ quarts.

SPOON'S BANANA ICE CREAM

4 eggs
2 cups sugar
½ teaspoon salt
2 teaspoons vanilla
1 13-ounce can evaporated
  milk

1 quart heavy cream
2 cups over-ripe bananas,
  mashed
milk

Beat eggs, slowly adding sugar and salt. Add vanilla, evaporated milk, cream, bananas, and enough milk to make 1 gallon; mix thoroughly. Freeze in electric freezer.

The trick is to use very brown bananas. Yields 1 gallon.

ELI'S ON EAST LTD.
Charlotte

ELI'S ON EAST LTD. Eli's on East Ltd. is in a house that has stood proud in the heart of Charlotte's Dilworth section since 1910. The stunning decoration gives the appearance of someone's ultra chic home rather than a restaurant, but a restaurant it is. The interior of Eli's reminds me of various flavors of sherbet, with their soft but richly colored shades.

Eli's was named after the great-grandfather of its proprietor, Robert Smoots. Smoots's wife, Karen, wanted to name their restaurant Dolly's of Dilworth because of its modish similarity to the era of *Hello Dolly*, but she was dissuaded when Smoots explained, "All the men will come for the first two weeks, then after they figure out it's only a restaurant, they'll never return."

Of course they would have returned after tasting the food, which is served with great panache. I mean it's hard not to be dazzled by a baked Alaska flambéed in a garden pot with fresh flowers erupting through the meringue. It is equally difficult not to respond to a strolling Dixieland band during brunch on Sunday. This is what makes Eli's a restaurant to put on your list. Reservations are a must for dinner. One man became so frustrated by the restaurant's continuous busy signal that he actually sent a telegram requesting reservations for that evening.

My first visit was for lunch, which is not by reservation. After the taste-teasing Welsh rarebit appetizer, which was on the house, I "semi-dieted" on the famous Cobb salad. It is attractively arranged in corn-row strips of chicken, onion, tomatoes, bacon, bleu cheese, and green peas on a bed of lettuce. I chose the house dressing, which is a pleasing mustard-based vinaigrette blend that perfectly accented the scrumptious salad. The butter-saturated rolls still cause me to salivate just by remembering them, but dessert was the real killer. I couldn't decide between the french-fried ice cream and the peanut butter pie, so I splurged on both and was not one bit sorry.

Dinner specialties recommended by friends are Veal Piquante or stuffed flounder, but next time I'm going to try the Russian Pavlov Burger, or if calories have gotten the worst of me, I'll happily settle for the fresh fruit served in a huge glass goblet.

I was amused to learn that the green latticework porch and garden were not original to the house. They were added because Charlotte's liquor law forbids people to be seen drinking. No matter; it is a lovely retreat where you may enjoy a sampling from the fine wine list or perhaps the restaurant's unique variation on a Bloody Mary.

I would wish you "Bon appétit," but Eli's is such a delectable adventure, I'll amend that to "Bon voyage!"

Eli's on East Ltd. is located at 311 East Boulevard in Charlotte. Lunch is served from 11:30 a. m. to 2:30 p. m., and dinner from 5:30 to 11:00 p. m., Tuesday through Saturday. Sunday brunch is served from 10:30 a. m. to 3:00 p. m. For reservations call (704) 375–0756.

ELI'S ON EAST LTD.'S GAZPACHO

4 tomatoes
1 cucumber
1 green pepper
3 to 4 green onions
2 No. 5 cans tomato juice
3 cloves garlic, crushed

¼ cup beef base or 1½ cups beef stock (see Index)
1 cup red wine vinegar
½ cup salad oil
4 teaspoons salt
¼ teaspoon Tabasco

4 teaspoons Worcestershire sauce

In steam kettle or Dutch oven, heat tomato juice to boiling. Peel cucumber and chop with other vegetables. Add the beef base or stock, crushed garlic, and all the vegetables; stir until well mixed. Stir in the vinegar, salad oil, salt, Worcestershire sauce, and Tabasco. Remove from kettle and refrigerate.

Serve with 7 or 8 croutons as a garnish. Serve hot or cold. Yields 1 gallon.

ELI'S ON EAST LTD.'S RASPBERRY SOUFFLÉ

2 envelopes unflavored
  gelatin
½ cup fresh lemon
  juice
8 eggs, separated
1 cup sugar

1 cup puréed fresh raspberries or well-drained
  frozen
4 tablespoons cassis, or
  2 tablespoons brandy and
  2 tablespoons currant
  jelly

2 cups heavy cream

Prepare a 2-quart soufflé dish with a waxed-paper collar extending 2 to 3 inches above rim of dish. Oil dish and paper.

Soften gelatin in lemon juice and heat over a low flame until light and fluffy. Add raspberries, cassis, and sugar to beaten egg yolks. Add gelatin and cook over hot water until thickened. While mixture cools, beat egg whites until stiff peaks form; whip cream until stiff. Gently fold egg whites into raspberry mixture, then fold in whipped cream. Pour into the soufflé dish and chill.

Remove collar just before serving. Serves 4 to 6.

ELI'S ON EAST LTD.'S PEANUT BUTTER PIE

2½ cups milk
1 cup sugar, brown or white
⅓ cup or less cornstarch
2 eggs
pinch of salt
1 teaspoon butter

1 cup peanut butter
1 teaspoon vanilla
1 deep 9-inch pie shell,
  baked
whipped cream
chopped peanuts

Bring milk to boiling point. In a bowl, mix sugar, cornstarch, eggs, salt, and butter. Slowly stir hot milk into egg mixture. Pour contents of bowl into saucepan and boil a few seconds. Add peanut butter and vanilla, and blend well. Pour in pie crust and cool.

Top with whipped cream and peanuts.

NICKLEBY'S
Charlotte

NICKLEBY'S

Nickleby's, a restaurant styled in the tradition of an old English tavern, is oddly sympatico with the Tuscan architecture of the home of the late Blanche Reynolds. In fact, Nickleby's is exactly the type of lucky admixture that occurs when one has the tastes, talents, and vision of Charles and Marian Tucker, the restaurant's current owners.

That is not to say that the Tuckers didn't have a challenge in the conversion of the 1926 house to their restaurant. Even replacing some of the terra-cotta roof tiles was a difficult job, since each tile was different. Each had been individually shaped over a man's thigh.

The house has many marvelous eccentricities, such as a room on the top floor that was once painted a metallic silver and is said to have been used for holding seances. Also in the room is an innocent-looking bookcase, which, when pressed at the right point, becomes a disappearing panel opening into a secret room. Isn't this the material that movies are made from?

The top floor is not open to the public; however, one can see elsewhere that the Tuckers have used the house's architectural quirks to their advantage. By blending the best of the furnishings from the sixteenth- and nineteenth-century restaurants they owned in England, they have created an atmosphere that is all their own.

A sweep of rich red carpeting now carries you from the entrance, past the red silk room and the hunt room, and down a curving stairway into the main dining room. There you are immediately aware of Nicholas Nickleby's imposing presence: the room is dominated by a five-foot portrait of the character from Charles Dickens' novel of the same name. It highlights the subtle elegance of the decor, which includes brass chandeliers and period oak furnishings.

Dieting, I had Nickleby's tossed salad with the broiled Dover sole for lunch, and I would recommend that even to those who aren't counting calories. A more ambitious lunch is the mixed grill, which consists of a steak, a lamb chop, an English sausage, bacon, and an egg. Although Nickleby's dinner menu offers either English or American dishes, I prefer the typically English roast beef or steak and oyster pie, with Yorkshire pudding and a sherry trifle for dessert.

The oak lounge, with paneling patterned from the house's original oak doors, offers a relaxing invitation before dinner. As might be expected at an English tavern, there is a bountiful selection of British beers and ales, as well as thirty-six different wines.

Anytime you are dining at Nickleby's becomes a special experience, but that is particularly so after 10 p.m., when your appetite beckons for a special "English snack." At those hours, it can only be found at Nickleby's.

Nickleby's is located at 715 Providence Road in Charlotte. Lunch is served from 11:30 a.m. to 2:30 p.m. and dinner from 6:00 to 10:00 p.m. Monday through Saturday. The lounge is open from 5:00 p.m. to midnight. For reservations call (704) 376–6180.

NICKLEBY'S BAKEWELL TART

1 recipe short crust pastry
  (see Index)
7½ tablespoons butter
7½ tablespoons sugar
2 eggs
⅛ cup plain flour, sieved

7½ tablespoons almond
  paste
5 tablespoons cake crumbs
2 tablespoons milk
3 tablespoons apricot
  preserves
powdered sugar

Roll pastry out thin and line a 7-inch flan ring. Cream butter and sugar together; beat in eggs; and fold in flour. Break up almond paste with a fork and beat into mixture. Add cake crumbs and milk. Spread apricot preserves over the bottom of the flan case. Place filling on the top of preserves, spreading evenly. Bake at 375 degrees for 30 to 40 minutes.

Cool and dust with powdered sugar. Serves 6.

NICKLEBY'S STEAK AND OYSTER PIE

1 recipe pie pastry (see
  Index)
1½ pounds stewing steak
1 pound oysters
flour for dredging
salt and pepper

1½ cups beef stock (see
  Index)
½ cup red wine
1 egg
1 tablespoon milk

Prepare pastry and roll it out. Refrigerate. Cut meat into small pieces and dredge in seasoned flour. Put in large deep-dish pie plate. Roll oysters in seasoned flour and add to meat. Mix stock with wine and add to meat, filling dish half-way. Cover pie with pastry, using leftover pastry pieces to fashion leaves. Combine milk and egg and brush over pie crust. Cut slits in pie and bake at 425 degrees for 15 minutes. Lower heat to 325 degrees, cover with aluminum foil, and continue baking for about 90 minutes. Serves 4.

NICKLEBY'S FISH STEW

1¼ pounds white fish
2 carrots
1 leek, or 1 medium onion
1 stick celery
2 pints fish fumet (see
  Index), or water
2 teaspoons salt

½ teaspoon pepper
1 bay leaf
pinch of thyme
½ stick butter
¼ cup flour
1 cup milk
1 egg yolk

½ cup heavy cream

Cut fish into small cubes; dice vegetables. Heat stock or water; add herbs, spices, vegetables, and fish. Simmer for 10 minutes. Meanwhile, make a thick sauce of the butter, flour, and milk. When hot and all lumps are incorporated, add strained fish stock and bring to a boil. Cook until thick; add vegetables and fish. Blend egg yolk with cream and stir into mixture. Heat through and serve. Do not boil. Serves 6 to 8.

THE COUNTRY INN
Matthews

THE COUNTRY INN What we have come to think of as "country food" is not what is served at the The Country Inn of Matthews.

An ancient magnolia tree stands at the entrance of this periwinkle blue farmhouse, which was built in 1890 by William Cecil Black. As the name implies, it has been decorated to resemble an old country inn, with blue-and-white plaid wallpaper. Absent, I am glad to say, are the dooddads that some decorators overuse in interiors of this period. On one wall, however, is a cross-stitched motto regarding the importance of family, which I felt was appropriate in this family-operated restaurant. As the restaurant's owner, Ray Lurz, jokingly said, the inn was "my wife's dream and my nightmare." Their daughter works part-time as a waitress, and their son, David, is the chef.

The menu reflects the influence of Lurz's home state in the Maryland-style crab cake. This was a new experience for me, and one that I eagerly recommend. The gold medal, however, has to go to the Mud Pie, which is superb. Dieters should definitely skip the pie and cobblers and take advantage of the vegetarian dish, which contains sautéed mushrooms, peppers, onions, and spinach. For dinner you could diet on prime rib, or if not on the calorie wagon, you could choose stuffed shrimp, turkey, or a marinated chicken breast.

No alcoholic beverages are offered; instead, a chilled glass of apple cider begins the meal. Or, if you wander in during the winter, you will be welcomed with the aroma of hot spiced cider, which will make you think you're back in your childhood again.

My visit was on a late-winter day, and I'm looking forward to returning again in the summer, when that old blue porch is abloom with baskets of geraniums and begonias. Next time I'll opt for the evening hour, when Mrs. Lurz entertains guests by playing old favorites on her piano. Once a youngster told her, "This is gettin' to be my favorite place to eat 'cause I just love your homemade music."

The Country Inn is located at 341 Ames Street in Matthews. Lunch is served from 11:30 a. m. to 2:00 p. m. Monday through Friday, and dinner from 5:30 to 9:00 p. m. Monday through Saturday. For reservations call (704) 847–1447.

THE COUNTRY INN'S
BROILED BARBECUED SHRIMP

1 pound large shrimp,
  shelled and deveined
¼ cup vegetable oil
⅓ cup chopped onions
1 cup bottled chili sauce
2 tablespoons brown sugar

⅓ cup lemon juice
2 tablespoons
  Worcestershire sauce
2 teaspoons prepared
  mustard
½ teaspoon salt

Heat oil and sauté onions until transparent. Add all other ingredients except shrimp; cover and simmer for 10 minutes. Arrange shrimp in foil-lined pan. Pour sauce over shrimp, and broil 3 inches from heat for 5 to 8 minutes. Serves 8.

THE COUNTRY INN'S BAKED BROCCOLI

2 packages frozen chopped
  broccoli
2 eggs, well beaten
1 cup grated medium-sharp
  cheddar cheese

1 can cream of mushroom
  soup
⅓ cup mayonnaise
1 teaspoon onion salt

Cook broccoli. Mix all ingredients together and place in a greased pan. Bake at 350 degrees for 30 minutes or until well set. Serves 6 to 8.

THE COUNTRY INN'S OVEN-CRISP CHICKEN

4 chicken breasts, deboned
¼ cup sour cream
1¼ teaspoons lemon juice

½ teaspoon garlic salt
¾ teaspoon celery salt
salt and pepper

139

1 teaspoon Worcestershire
  sauce
1 teaspoon paprika

1 cup herb-seasoned
  stuffing mix
½ stick butter, melted

Mix sour cream, lemon juice, and seasonings. Dip chicken into mixture and roll in stuffing mix. Arrange chicken in greased shallow baking dish. Brush with melted butter. Bake uncovered at 350 degrees for 1 hour or until done. Serves 4.

THE COUNTRY INN'S CRAB CAKES

1 pound back fin crabmeat
  (pick out shells carefully)
2 slices bread
¼ cup milk
¼ teaspoon salt
1 egg, beaten
1 teaspoon Old Bay
  Seasoning

1 tablespoon mayonnaise
1 tablespoon Worcestershire
  sauce
1 tablespoon chopped
  parsley
2 tablespoons margarine

Remove crusts from bread and break into small pieces; moisten with milk. Mix all ingredients except margarine, and shape into large, flat cakes. Fry in margarine until light brown on both sides. Serves 4 to 6.

THE COUNTRY INN'S MUD PIE

1 16-ounce can chocolate
  syrup
1 graham cracker crust

1 quart Baskin Robbins
  Jamoca Almond Fudge ice
  cream

whipped cream

Pour a layer of chocolate syrup to barely cover bottom of pie crust. Add ice cream and drizzle remaining chocolate syrup on top. Place in freezer until it hardens.

Remove and top with whipped cream. Serves 6.

SCHEIBERS JOLLY MILL
RESTAURANT
Elkin

**SCHEIBERS JOLLY
MILL RESTAURANT**

Every time man tries to improve upon nature, he loses something—something important." That is the philosophy that Stefan Scheibers, an Austrian-born naturalist, brings into the kitchen of his Jolly Mill Restaurant. Scheibers believes that food is at its best when fresh, without preservatives, and as my grandmother used to say, "made from scratch."

When Scheibers decided to transform his 1896 mill into a restaurant, he chose to salvage the pine flooring and beams, which have been held intact with the same wooden pegs for all these years. Visitors are invited to the upper loft, where the mill's machinery has been retained in the areas where it was first installed. As you walk through the rooms downstairs, which are decorated with bits of antique embroidery, lace curtains, and various old and new crafts comfortably arranged on cupboards and washstands, you will be viewing the work of Scheibers' wife, Nancy, whom he describes as "an artist all the way."

The gushing water you will hear running over the rocks beside the mill is the Big Elkin Creek, and until a few years ago this water was the source of power for the old flour mill. Scheibers wishes it were possible to use that natural energy, but damaging floods have destroyed the dam and turbine, and the cost of a rebuilding project is prohibitive at present.

Even so, the lulling sound of water sweeping past you adds an element of tranquility to a meal of butterflied shrimp in Champagne batter, rounded off with Scheibers' scrumptious Austrian apple strudel. Obviously, I wasn't dieting when I ate that, but had I been so inclined, I could have had Trout Amandine or veal in lemon sauce. My friend ordered the Veal Cordon Bleu, which was made with country ham and Swiss cheese, and she almost licked her plate clean. She, who is always on a diet, was so relaxed by the atmosphere that she went right on to have an Austrian torte prepared by one of Scheibers' three adopted sons.

In his charming Southern-textured Austrian accent, Scheibers proudly told of the Saturday his family grew from zero to three. It seems that he and his wife went to pick up forty pounds of trout and returned with a baby boy in diapers. Within five months the boy was joined by his two natural brothers. Every time the social worker called to ask if they would take another son, he answered, "Yah, we take them all."

So, if you're visiting the mill on Sunday, your dessert may be prepared by the Scheibers' fourteen-year-old, who is beginning his apprenticeship at the same age his father did. The difference is that the new generation prefers to start with desserts. I can understand that.

The Jolly Mill is located on Carter Mill Road off U.S. 21 Business north of Elkin. Lunch is served from 11:30 a.m. to 1:30 p.m. Wednesday and Thursday, and dinner from 5:00 to 9:00 p.m. Wednesday through Sunday. For reservations call (919) 835-7720.

JOLLY MILL'S SHRIMP SPECIAL

1 pound large shrimp, shelled and deveined
2 eggs, separated
1 cup self-rising flour
1 cup champagne or beer
1 teaspoon sugar
pinch of basil
pinch of tarragon
pinch of salt
oil for frying

Mix egg yolks into flour; stir in champagne or beer until the consistency of pancake batter. Add sugar and seasonings, mixing well. In separate bowl beat egg whites until stiff and fold very carefully into batter. Cut shrimp down center to give butterfly effect. Dip shrimp in batter and place in one inch or more of oil at 300 degrees. Fry until golden brown.

Serve on bed of rice pilaf with creole sauce (see recipe below). Serves 3 to 4.

JOLLY MILL'S CREOLE SAUCE

1 onion, chopped
2 green peppers, chopped
2 tablespoons butter
½ cup red wine

2 cups peeled and chopped
   tomatoes
½ cup ketchup
2 tablespoons tomato paste
   water

Sauté onion and peppers in butter; add wine and tomatoes. Stir in ketchup and tomato paste, mixing thoroughly. Add enough water to provide smooth consistency.
Serve over shrimp. Serves 4.

JOLLY MILL'S APPLE STRUDEL

puff pastry (Pepperidge
   Farm)
2 large apples, peeled
   and sliced
1½ tablespoons sugar
⅓ teaspoon vanilla
2 tablespoons raisins
1 tablespoon lemon juice

dash of cloves
dash of cinnamon
⅓ cup grated lemon rind
⅓ cup grated orange rind
½ cup bread crumbs
⅛ cup cream
1 egg white, beaten
confectioners' sugar

On floured board, roll out pastry to ⅛-inch thick and cut into 2 rectangles 6 inches by 10 inches. Combine apples, sugar, vanilla, raisins, lemon juice, spices, and citrus peels. Place bread crumbs on pastry to form a line down the center, then place strudel filling on top of crumbs. Pour cream over filling. Fold ends and then sides. Seal the seams with egg whites. Put on greased baking tray and bake at 350 degrees for 45 minutes. Sprinkle with powdered sugar.
Serve hot with vanilla ice cream. Serves 4 to 6.

SHATLEY SPRINGS INN
Crumpler

SHATLEY SPRINGS INN

Perhaps the food at Shatley Springs Inn is the principal drawing card today, but that was not always the case. The inn began in the early part of the century as a health resort.

The story concerning the origin of Shatley Springs Inn is recounted in a printed statement by Martin Shatley. He claims that for over seven years he had been so ill with consumption and other painful diseases that doctors pronounced him incurable. Believing that he was near death, Shatley bought a farm to provide for his family's welfare. Soon after the purchase of the farm, Shatley passed a spring on his land and stopped to bathe his inflamed face. He declared that in less than an hour the healing process had begun. After only a few days of bathing in the spring water, his fever disappeared, and in three weeks, he was well enough to do heavy farm labor. His statement further asserts that in the ensuing thirty-five years he witnessed the cure of people with skin diseases, rheumatism, and nervous disorders.

I was curious to see the spring providing these curative waters, which according to analysts is especially high in calcium, magnesium, and five other healthful minerals. But the aroma of fried chicken drew me into the dining room.

The man sitting next to my table said, "I bet you could have a good meal by eating the crumbs off this table." That expression intrigued me, but it wasn't long before my own table was crammed to the limit with dishes of food served "family style." Shatley Springs offers what I would describe as country food that has been properly seasoned. Diners can choose among several entrées, and my favorite is the chicken pie. The cooks at Shatley vow that there isn't a cookbook or written recipe on the place, thus making it impractical for them to break down the recipes for me to test for an average-sized family. The fried chicken recipe is so secret that a waitress told me her mother had worked at Shatley for years and still didn't know it. The country hams are cured by the restaurant's co-owners, the McMillans, who sell them whole and by the pound, as well as by the plateful.

I did discover the secret that makes the vegetables tastier than mine. Those at Shatley are fresh or frozen and are cooked with half-and-half, real butter, and a little flour. What a difference the real thing can make. This just doesn't seem the type of place you'd think of for a dieter, but I was surprised that a cottage cheese and fresh fruit salad is available for lunch.

Saturday nights frequently feature country, bluegrass, or gospel music; but alcoholic beverages are never allowed. That philosophy seems in harmony with the healing minerals of the spring outside. Even today people come from distant states to haul away the mystical waters. There is no charge for the water, but a nominal fee is collected for an unused plastic gallon jug to take it home in.

After my plentiful meal I was feeling no pain at all, but you never know what's in store, do you? So, yes, I brought home a gallon of Shatley Spring's water for, well, just in case.

Shatley Springs Inn is located on N. C. 16 at Crumpler. It is open from 7:00 a. m. to 9:00 p. m. seven days a week, May through October. For reservations call (919) 982–2236.

SHATLEY SPRINGS INN'S COLESLAW

1 head cabbage	**½ cup mayonnaise**
¼ cup diced onion	**2 tablespoons vinegar**
½ cup milk	**½ teaspoon salt**
¼ cup sugar	**½ teaspoon pepper**

Shred cabbage. Add other ingredients and correct seasoning to taste.

Cover and refrigerate. Serves 4.

SHATLEY SPRINGS INN'S CREAMED POTATOES

8 potatoes, peeled and   ½ stick butter
  quartered   1 tablespoon or more flour
1 teaspoon salt   2 cups half-and-half

In medium pot, place potatoes, salt, and water to cover. Boil until potatoes are tender; drain. Add butter, half-and-half, flour, and mix until smooth and thick.

Serve hot. Serves 6 to 8.

SHATLEY SPRINGS INN'S RHUBARB COBBLER

2 cups chopped rhubarb   1 teaspoon lemon juice
pinch of salt   2 tablespoons butter
1 cup sugar   brown sugar
½ teaspoon cinnamon   1 handful fresh
¼ teaspoon nutmeg   strawberries, cut up
          1 pie crust, unbaked (see Index)

In covered saucepan, boil rhubarb in salted water until tender. Drain and place in greased shallow baking dish. Mix together sugar, cinnamon, nutmeg, and lemon juice; mix with rhubarb. Dot with butter and sprinkle with strawberries. Cover with rolled-out pie crust and sprinkle brown sugar on top. Bake at 350 degrees about 40 minutes or until done. Serves 8 to 10.

GREENFIELD RESTAURANT
West Jefferson

**GREENFIELD
RESTAURANT**

As I sat sipping my coffee and gazing through a bay window at rolling green fields, I could easily understand how this rustic restaurant got its name. A moment later I was eating an overabundant breakfast of country ham, sausage, eggs, grits, gravy, strawberry preserves, and a batch of biscuits so good that they literally sent me into the kitchen for the recipe. Now I know why mountain people are so robust and healthy. Their plentiful natural resources sponsor these attributes.

Those natural resources were first recognized by the Cherokee Indians, who used a nearby spring and sheltered themselves inside a cave on Mount Jefferson. The cave, still rich in Indian artifacts, was discovered several years ago. Old-timers of the region remember the covered wagons that sought refuge near the natural spring, where milk and butter were kept cool in a deep trough. It was nearby that Rufus McNeil built the white farmhouse that is now Greenfield. The date of the house, 1890, remains chiseled inside the fireplace.

During the McNeils' tenure, the land was used to farm, and chestnuts and chinquapins were gathered from the woods. Today, however, farming has been replaced by a full-scale recreation area. In addition to being served three meals a day at Greenfield, you can go camping, canoe, ride horseback, hike, and swim. On alternate Saturday nights in the summer, you are welcome to attend an evening of square dancing or bluegrass music.

I am also pleased to report that Greenfield is another of the country-style restaurants where you can have a light fresh fruit salad or the Greenfield vegetable salad for lunch. The management is happy to comply with your dietary requirements at dinner if you give them notice before you go. However, most people go to Greenfield for the fried chicken, country ham, and the other simple, old-fashioned foods for which the restaurant is so famous. Once during dinner, the parking lot was packed not only with cars and motorcycles, but with two firetrucks, a helicopter, two horses, and a boat.

A local reporter remarked, "People will come here by just about any mode of transportation that runs." After only one meal I can say "amen" to that remark.

Greenfield Restaurant is located three miles south of West Jefferson, off U. S. 221 and N. C. 163. It is open for three meals a day from 7:30 a. m. to 9:30 p. m. seven days a week, from April 1 through December 23. For reservations call (919) 246–9671.

GREENFIELD'S BEAN CASSEROLE

1 can kidney beans	1 green pepper, chopped
1 can wax beans	1 large onion, chopped
1 can green beans	½ cup light brown sugar
1 can baby limas	½ cup ketchup
1 can pork and beans	salt and pepper

Drain all beans except pork and beans. Mix all ingredients and place in a greased casserole. Bake at 350 degrees for about 45 minutes. Serves 12 to 14.

GREENFIELD'S BISCUITS

2 cups Southern Biscuit self-rising flour	1 tablespoon sugar
⅔ cup buttermilk	1 teaspoon baking powder
⅔ cup sweet milk	⅓ cup margarine
	⅓ cup shortening

Mix flour, milk, sugar, and baking powder. Work margarine and shortening into flour mixture. Cover well and refrigerate. Will keep for a day.

Roll out on floured board and cut out with biscuit cutter. Bake at 450 degrees for 8 to 10 minutes. Yields 12 biscuits.

GREENFIELD'S RICE AND PINEAPPLE

3 cups uncooked white rice
1 stick margarine, melted
1 cup sugar

1 No. 2 can (2½ cups)
   crushed pineapple
1 teaspoon salt

Cook rice; mix in margarine. Add sugar, pineapple, and salt, and mix well.

Serve hot. Serves 8 to 10.

GLENDALE SPRINGS INN
Glendale Springs

GLENDALE
SPRINGS INN

Why would a Broadway producer want to open a gourmet restaurant in an 1895 inn in Glendale Springs? The atmosphere in Glendale Springs is not the same as New York's; the people are not the same; the landscape is not the same. The fact of the matter is that those differences provided the motivating factor for Gayle Winston to bid on General Adams' inn when it was auctioned.

When she learned that the house was to be auctioned off in pieces, Ms. Winston couldn't stand it. She had had no intention of buying it, but she couldn't bear to see something so fine dismembered. Not even knowing if she could finance the project, she asked the owners if they would accept a bad check until she could make more solid arrangements. They did, and she did, and the result is reminiscent of an exquisite piece of antique jewelry that has been polished and replaced in its familiar setting, and now proudly radiates its original elegance.

A large measure of this elegance cannot be attributed so much to the physical beauty of the inn; it comes, rather, from the remembrance that nineteenth-century society was based on the values of good taste. This taste is evidenced in so many ways at the inn, from the white linen tablecloths dressed with fresh flowers, to the iced tea served in wine glasses, to the properly schooled service. These elements coalesce to produce an aura so distinctive that you will expect no less than epicurean food. And, in my opinion, you will not be disappointed.

At lunch, the zucchini soup with fresh herbs in a cream sauce was analogous to a full-bodied wine. It was followed by a light salad of greens and hearts of palm with a tiny violet perched in the center. The reason the asparagus omelet was so special was the fresh asparagus and fresh country eggs. Ever notice the difference a fresh egg makes? My dessert of grapefruit and kir sorbets was the most refreshing experience of the entire meal. To be on the fair side, I did conduct a taste-test of the coffee almond torte and the triple chocolate Napoleon, which are top candidates for any chocoholic.

The most popular appetizer for dinner is a deep-fried herbed crepe filled with Gruyère cheese, and this may be followed by a unique tomato vichyssoise. The most unusual entrée is the veal with bacon, herbs, and red wine in puff pastry. If you are in the mood for a lighter meal, the rainbow trout would be an excellent choice.

The inn has a "special occasion" license, meaning that wine and other alcoholic beverages can be arranged prior to your meal. Any time that you dine or overnight at the inn will be a special occasion because history and good taste have made it so. The inn is one block from the fresco of the Last Supper at Holy Trinity Episcopal Church.

Glendale Springs Inn is located on N.C. 16 at Glendale Springs. It is open for lunch from 12:00 to 2:00 p.m. and for dinner from 6:00 to 9:00 p.m. Wednesday through Sunday, from May through October. For reservations call (919) 982–2102.

GLENDALE SPRINGS INN'S HERB BUTTER

1 stick butter	1 teaspoon chopped chives
2 tablespoons chopped	2 shallots, chopped
fresh tarragon	6 parsley sprigs

Combine ingredients in food processor with steel blade or use electric mixer.

GLENDALE SPRINGS INN'S ZUCCHINI SOUP

1 large onion, chopped	2 cups vegetable broth or
2 cloves garlic, minced	beef stock (see Index)
2 tablespoons herb butter	2 cups half-and-half
(see recipe above)	2 tablespoons curry powder
4 cups zucchini, peeled	
and sliced thin	

155

Sauté onions and garlic in herb butter. Cover and let sweat for 1 minute. Add zucchini and vegetable broth or beef stock. Cover and cook until tender. Drain and puree in blender. Return to saucepan and add half-and-half and curry. Heat through. Serves 8.

GLENDALE SPRINGS INN'S
ASPARAGUS OMELET

8 to 10 asparagus spears	dash of fresh-ground
melted lemon butter	nutmeg
salt	milk
3 eggs	fresh Hollandaise sauce
dash of fresh-ground	(see Index)
pepper	parsley

Steam asparagus; cut into one-inch pieces and drizzle with melted lemon butter and a sprinkle of salt. Set aside and keep warm. Lightly mix eggs, nutmeg, salt, pepper, and milk. Melt butter in an omelet skillet and pour in egg mixture. With the back of a fork, lightly scramble the eggs. As soon as mixture begins to set, add asparagus to center and fold egg over asparagus. Divide into two equal portions and place on warm plates. Dress with a ribbon of freshly prepared Hollandaise sauce and garnish with parsley. Serves 2.

GLENDALE SPRINGS INN'S
GRAPEFRUIT SORBET

4 or more grapefruits	1 cup water
	2 cups sugar

Squeeze 3 cups grapefruit juice and set aside. Place water and sugar in a small saucepan and bring to a rolling boil; cook until it forms a simple syrup. Add syrup to grapefruit juice and mix. Cover tightly and put in freezer.

When firmly chilled, place in ice cream freezer and follow machine's instructions. You may freeze mixture in freezer for different consistency. Yields 10 to 12 scoops.

DAN'L BOONE INN
Boone

DAN'L BOONE INN 	 After eating at the Dan'l Boone Inn, it's amazing that I can even spell the word "diet." I ate with complete disregard of its meaning. I'll bet if such food had been served back in 1919, when this rambling old edifice operated as a hospital, poor appetites would have completely disappeared.

"Oh, but the food is embarrassingly simple," protested one of the inn's co-owners, Jim Paal, when I asked for his recipes. "It's nothing more than your mother prepares at home. But our box lunch is a real buy. When it's warmer, people take these boxes to a picnic table in the garden. That way they can escape the long lines and also enjoy the folk and country bands." Just for the record, that simple box contains two pieces of chicken, green beans, stewed apples, two homemade country ham biscuits, two plain biscuits, home-baked cake, and a beverage. I can assure you that my mother never packed me a box lunch like that!

I would have liked to dine on the porch, which has a tree growing through its center, but the comforting stone fireplace in the knotty-pine dining room has more appeal on a winter day. The room, with its sagging floors, is decorated with an assemblage of functioning antiques that range from apple presses to clocks.

The waitress served us family-style, which means that the entire menu was placed upon our red tablecloth in bowls or platters, including three different meats. That allows a choice of whatever and how much you want to eat. My vote goes to the country style steak, black cherry preserves on hot biscuits, and prune cake for dessert. Though not recommended for dieters, the Dan'l Boone does offer a vegetarian meal at a reduced price.

After dark, the entertainment moves inside, and it isn't unusual to find customers joining in the singing or dancing. This is the kind of place where total strangers are apt to become well acquainted before the close of an evening.

The Dan'l Boone Inn is located at 105 Hardin Street in Boone. The inn is open in summer from 11:00 a.m. to 9:00 p.m. Monday through Friday, and from 7:00 a.m. to 9:00 p.m. Saturday and Sunday. The schedule varies through the winter. Reservations are not necessary, but for information call (704) 264-8657.

DAN'L BOONE INN'S STEWED APPLES

5 McIntosh apples   ½ cup sugar
¾ stick butter or margarine

Wash apples thoroughly. Core and section, and wash again. Melt butter in large, heavy pot. Place apples and sugar in pot; stew on high for a couple of minutes, then cook at medium high until soft but not mushy, about 8 minutes. (Add no water or other spices.) Serves 3 to 4.

DAN'L BOONE INN'S CRANBERRY RELISH

1 12-ounce package fresh   3 large oranges
  cranberries   2 16-ounce cans jellied
10 apples   cranberries

Grate fresh cranberries coarse and grate apples fine. (Can use food processor for this.) Dice peeled orange, removing any seeds. Mix all ingredients. Cover and refrigerate for 24 hours.

This will keep from Thanksgiving through Christmas. Yields 1½ quarts.

DAN'L BOONE INN'S PRUNE CAKE

2 cups sugar   1 teaspoon nutmeg
1 cup vegetable oil   1 teaspoon allspice
3 eggs   1 teaspoon cinnamon
2 cups self-rising flour   1 junior-size jar of
⅓ cup dry buttermilk   baby food prunes
                1 cup chopped nuts

Mix sugar and oil; beat in eggs. Add flour, buttermilk, nutmeg, allspice, and cinnamon. Blend together well. Stir in prunes and nuts. Bake in greased bundt pan or tube pan at 325 degrees for 1 hour and 15 minutes.

Frost with buttermilk icing.

DAN'L BOONE INN'S BUTTERMILK ICING

⅓ cup buttermilk
½ stick margarine

1 cup brown sugar
1 box confectioners' sugar

Mix the buttermilk, margarine, and brown sugar; bring to a boil. Slowly mix in the confectioners' sugar. Blend thoroughly.

Cool cake and frosting before spreading.

GREEN PARK INN
Blowing Rock

GREEN PARK INN

Prepare to be pleasurably pampered when you enter the Victorian-style Green Park Inn, with its abundance of latticework and white wicker furniture. Even in the winter the lobby resembles a burst of spring, with its bright green and yellow flowered decor. The green is, of course, symbolic of the Green family, whose seven brothers built their inn a hundred years ago right on the Eastern Continental Divide.

The lounge, called The Divide, is bisected by the line. It is one of the enhancing additions that came with the inn's renovation in 1977. I was heartened to see that the renovators were careful to retain the charming traditions that reigned during the South's era of graciousness, particularly in the multi-leveled dining room. There, dark green velvet chairs and white damask tablecloths are positioned at one end of the dance floor, where weekend dancing is enjoyed to the tunes of bygone days, as well as to those of the present time.

Since the menu changes daily, it is difficult to know which of Red Bettencourt's offerings of steak, chicken, pork, seafood, homemade soups, fresh vegetables, home-baked rolls, and salads will appeal to you. I thought the stuffed pork chops and onion rolls were the best until, on another occasion, I found the Coq au Vin to be so magnificent that I persuaded Bettencourt to share the recipe with us. Obviously I wasn't dieting, because I went right on to coconut cake, which was better than my grandmother's.

The best time to enjoy the Green Park is during the celebrated Sunday buffet. It is the most dazzling array of gastronomical and visual delights around. Fresh flowers in an ice-sculpture vase grace tables of tempting morsels arranged in silver chafing dishes. Don't try to resist even one of the four tables that are laden with preparations responsible for fantasy dreaming. Everything is delicious, but the seafood salad is such a winner that repeat diners check to make sure it is on the agenda before making reservations. An important dividend is that the buffet easily accommodates most diets, or you can order broiled beef or seafood.

With the quality of food and splendor that are synonymous with Green Park, it isn't surprising that in the past hundred years the inn has given refuge to presidents from Wilson to Ford. This is a comfortable place where world leaders have been found playing cards in the kitchen with the chef.

Green Park Inn is located on U. S. 321 Bypass in Blowing Rock. Breakfast is served from 7:00 to 9:30 a. m., lunch from noon to 2:00 p. m., and dinner from 6:00 to 10:00 p. m. Sunday buffet is from noon to 3:00 p. m. For reservations call (704) 295–3141.

GREEN PARK INN'S SEAFOOD SALAD

¼ pound langostinos
¼ pound Alaskan shrimp
¼ pound Alaskan king crab
  or (Atlantic snow crab)
½ cup diced peeled celery
½ cup diced onions
juice of 1 lime
⅔ cup mayonnaise

¼ teaspoon white pepper
½ teaspoon salt
dash of Worcestershire
  sauce
bib lettuce
black olives
sliced lemons

Boil seafood; cool and squeeze water from seafood. Mix seafood, celery, onions, lime juice, and seasonings. Refrigerate.

Serve on lettuce and garnish with olives and lemon slices. Yields 1 pound.

GREEN PARK INN'S COQ AU VIN

2 chickens, cut-up
1 stick butter
1 dozen white mushrooms,
  capped

7 cups chicken stock
  (see Index)
½ cup flour
¼ cup good white wine

¼ pound salt pork   ¼ cup good brandy
1 cup tiny whole onions   1½ cups uncooked rice

Brown chicken in butter, and remove to baking dish. Sauté mushrooms, salt pork, and onions until transparent; add to chicken. Make gravy from butter, flour, and 4 cups chicken stock. Add wine and brandy, and bring to a boil. Strain gravy over chicken, mushrooms, onions, and salt pork. Cover with aluminium foil. Bake at 400 degrees for 45 minutes or until done.

Cook rice in 3 cups chicken stock. Serve chicken over rice. Serves 6 to 8.

GREEN PARK INN'S STUFFED PORK CHOPS

4 to 6 lean pork chops   1 sausage link
1 quart pork gravy   3 slices bacon, cooked
  (use 2 packages of mix)   ¼ cup diced celery
1 pound bread   ¼ cup diced onions
3 eggs   ½ teaspoon sage
1 cup chicken stock   salt and pepper
  (see Index)

Mix bread, eggs, chicken stock, sausage, bacon, celery, onions, and seasonings to make dressing. Slice pork chops in center but do not cut through; fill with dressing. Place in baking pan and cover with pork gravy. Cover with foil. Bake at 400 degrees for 45 to 60 minutes. Serves 4 to 6.

NU-WRAY INN
Burnsville

NU-WRAY INN

Protected in a pocket of the Blue Ridge Mountains is an 1833 inn whose original eight rooms were erected with logs and held together with locust pins. When you arrive at the Nu-Wray Inn, which has been in the Wray family for the past hundred years, it will take a moment to remember that you are still in the twentieth century. I am sure you will soon welcome the adjustment from the pre-packaged pleasures of the city to this oasis of gentility.

Comfortable rockers invite you to sit on the sprawling veranda, or you may meander past the parlor's stone fireplace to the upstairs drawing room known as the "Blue Room." Unlike many drab Colonial colors, the forget-me-not blue of the doors and mantel illumines the room's rich Victorian furniture and its assortment of musical instruments, not the least of which is a square rosewood piano and a Reginaphone music box.

Don't become so removed from time in the graciousness of this room that you miss the chime of the dinner bell, because the amount and variety of food set upon the lace-covered tables is reminiscent of a medieval banquet. My first visit was on Thanksgiving. Need I say more? Only a masochist could diet in the presence of those temptations. My family indulged, to speak euphemistically, in country ham, fried chicken, turkey, dressing, corn pudding, candied yams, relish, and mouth-watering hot biscuits dripping with butter and pear honey. Then we slipped in old-fashioned cakes and pies of every description. My favorites were sour cream pie and tipsy cake.

Later, when I asked what was enjoyed most, I received a chorus of "Everything!" In the summer you can diet on the smothered lettuce salad, but my advice is this: Enjoy the banquet and then hike for two to three hours, if you can still move.

The Nu-Wray Inn is located on the town square in Burnsville. Breakfast is served at 8:30 a.m., and supper at 6:30

p.m., Monday through Saturday. Sunday dinner is served from 12:30 to 2:00 p.m. For reservations call (704) 682–2329.

NU-WRAY INN'S SYLLABUB

1 quart cream, 24 hours old
1 cup fresh milk
1 cup sugar
1 teaspoon vanilla

½ cup grape juice, or
¼ cup orange juice
½ cup sherry

Chill all ingredients. Place in a large bowl, and beat with egg beater until frothy. Serve immediately. Serves 10.

NU-WRAY INN'S CREAM GRAVY

4 tablespoons bacon grease
3 tablespoons flour
½ teaspoon salt

½ cup milk
½ cup water

Heat bacon grease. Add flour and salt; stir until it begins to brown. Add milk and water, and boil until thick.
Serve with steamed rice. Yields 1 cup.

NU-WRAY INN'S SOUR CREAM PIE

1 cup sour cream
¾ cups sugar
2 eggs
pinch of salt
1 teaspoon cinnamon

½ teaspoon nutmeg
½ teaspoon ground cloves
1 9-inch pie shell, unbaked
½ cup chopped pecans
whipped cream

Mix sugar and sour cream together; add slightly beaten eggs, salt, and spices. Pour into unbaked pie shell and bake at 425 degrees for 8 to 10 minutes. Reduce heat to 325 degrees and bake another 20 minutes or more.

A cup of undiluted evaporated milk plus one tablespoon of vinegar may be used in place of sour cream.

Sweetened whipped cream and pecans may be placed on top.

NU-WRAY INN'S TIPSY CAKE

Cake:

3 eggs
1 cup sugar
4 tablespoons cold water

1½ cups flour
2 heaping teaspoons
baking powder

Custard:

1 quart milk
5 eggs, minus whites
of 2 eggs

5 tablespoons sugar
1 tablespoon cornstarch
1 teaspoon vanilla

Topping:

½ cup good wine,
such as sherry
½ pint whipping cream

2 egg whites
any red jelly
⅔ cup sliced almonds,
toasted

For the cake, sift flour and baking powder together twice. Beat eggs and sugar together until light; add water and flour alternately. Bake in two greased and floured cake pans at 350 degrees for 25 to 30 minutes.

For the custard, bring milk to a boil. Beat eggs. Mix eggs, sugar, and cornstarch into boiling milk. Remove from heat and stir in vanilla. Let cool until thick.

To assemble, place one layer of cake in a large, deep bowl and moisten with wine. Cover top with almonds; add half of boiled custard. Repeat with second layer. Whip cream with egg whites until stiff and pile high on last layer of cake. Place bits of red jelly on top.

NU-WRAY INN'S PEAR HONEY

7 pounds pears, nearly ripe
5 pounds sugar

1 large can shredded
pineapple

Peel and core pears. Put through largest hole of meat grinder or in food processor. Mix sugar with pears; boil 50 minutes, stirring toward the last to prevent sticking. Add pineapple and boil about 10 minutes longer, until syrup thickens. Seal in sterile jars.

Good on vanilla ice cream. Yields 8 to 9 pints.

WEAVERVILLE MILLING COMPANY
Weaverville

WEAVERVILLE MILLING CO.

Remember "Rosie the Riveter," the symbolic World War II woman who took the traditional male jobs that kept the factories producing while our boys were away? Weaverville Milling Company had its own version of Rosie in Margie Duff, who kept the mill wheel grinding out the community's flour and meal during the war years. It was an arduous task, but a combination of woman power and will power kept the operation going.

Weaverville Milling Company is now a restaurant, but remnants of the operation that began in 1912 can still be found on the top floor of the mill. The equipment now enhances the restaurant's rustic decor and sets the stage for a participatory look backward. Guests at the restaurant are free to do more than just have a good meal.

Near our table on the main floor was an old jigsaw puzzle. Every now and then a diner would wander over and fit another piece into its place. On the mezzanine, which is decorated with handmade quilts that are for sale, an old-fashioned dollhouse waits for the amusement of children before or after dinner.

Lovely touches of the country are everywhere. Just as we were returning to our seats from our tour, a woman placed on our table one of the loveliest bouquets of wildflowers you could imagine. The colors of the flowers set off our yellow-and-white checked tablecloth, the yellow pine walls, and the original oak floor.

The menu contained so many of my favorites that I had a hard time making a decision—until I found the chicken with raspberry and rhubarb sauce. What could be more unusual! The dish was so delicious that I tried to include the recipe here, but neither the chef nor I could figure out a way to break it down to family-size proportions.

My daughter Heather chose the very hearty V.I.P. Sandwich, prime rib au jus on toast with country fried potatoes. If you are trying to take it on the light side, the vegetarian lasagne might be a good suggestion, or fresh mountain trout broiled in a lemon and herb sauce.

Dieters beware: No meal at Weaverville would be complete without the desserts that have made the restaurant famous. They originated from old local recipes, but each has been given a creative twist. The freshest fruit of the season made the blueberry and peach cobbler a standout, especially when topped with homemade vanilla ice cream; but a taste of Heather's oatmeal pie—reminiscent of a pecan pie—made that recipe a must.

I declined the special wine of the day because the home-made apple juice seemed exactly appropriate to this home-spun experience. Guests under sixteen or over seventy-five receive a complimentary Slushy, an icy drink of 7-Up and grenadine. This is a terrific treat for all ages and will add a refreshing note to any hot summer day.

Weaverville Milling Company reminds me of an unpol-ished gem that turns up in a rock collector's pan: a treasure sparkling within a rough exterior.

Weaverville Milling Company is located on Reems Creek Road in Weaverville, ten minutes north of Asheville. Dinner is served from 5:00 to 9:00 p.m., daily except Wednesdays from April to December, and Thursday through Sunday in January, February, and March. For reservations call (704) 645-4700.

WEAVERVILLE MILLING COMPANY'S SLUSHY

6 ounces 7-Up   2 ounces club soda
1 tablespoon grenadine   6 ice cubes

Place all ingredients in blender and mix until frothy. Serves 1.

WEAVERVILLE MILLING COMPANY'S
PEACH AND BLUEBERRY COBBLER

2 cups fresh peaches, sliced   1 tablespoon lemon juice
1 cup fresh blueberries   1 cup flour
1 teaspoon cinnamon   1 teaspoon baking powder

½ teaspoon salt
3 tablespoons margarine,
   melted
1 cup white sugar

½ cup brown sugar
½ cup milk
1 tablespoon cornstarch
1 cup boiling water

Grease a 9- by 9-inch pan and fill with fruit. Sprinkle cinnamon and lemon juice over fruit. Mix flour, baking powder, and salt. Cream margarine, brown sugar, and ½ cup white sugar. Sift dry ingredients into creamed mixture, alternately adding milk; mix well. Spread over fruit. Sift ½ cup white sugar with cornstarch and sprinkle over batter. Pour boiling water over pie. Bake at 350 degrees for about an hour. Serves 8 to 10.

WEAVERVILLE MILLING COMPANY'S OATMEAL PIE

1 9-inch pie shell, unbaked
¼ cup margarine, melted
½ cup brown sugar
1 cup white corn syrup

1 cup raw oatmeal
3 eggs
½ teaspoon ground cloves
½ teaspoon cinnamon

¼ teaspoon salt

With electric mixer cream butter and sugar together; add all other ingredients and mix well. Pour into unbaked pie shell and bake at 350 degrees for approximately 1 hour.

GROVE PARK INN
Asheville

GROVE PARK INN The wind, for some reason, feels cleaner when it greets you on the high balcony of the Grove Park Inn. Perhaps blowing through the blue haze of the Smoky Mountains gives it a certain crispness. I don't know, but I can say that looking across at the mountains, with the city of Asheville tucked below, makes the word spectacular seem inadequate.

E. W. Grove must have had a similar attitude when he built this inn in 1913. Even today it is awesome to walk through the solid granite structure, which was literally hewed out of Sunset Mountain. Grove's philosophy of "thinking big" was part of his desire to create a hotel that would be considered the epitome of gracious hospitality. The original advertising for the inn proudly stated that "All our waiters wear freshly laundered white gloves," and "Guests are encouraged to speak in low tones." Grove Park was billed not as a sanatorium, but as "a resting place for tired people." Having just completed a long drive on one of my restaurant tours, I was the perfect applicant when I arrived there.

I lunched in the Dogwood Room on the opening day of the season, and I can't imagine either the food or the service being better. Sitting beside a panorama picture window that afforded the same breathtaking view as the balcony, I had a delicious cup of French onion soup and a bouquet of fresh fruits served with special yogurt-based dressing. What a scrumptious way to sabotage the calories! Though the dessert tray of French pastries was intriguing, I bravely passed up those enticements. A complete beer and wine list is available for both lunch and dinner. It features premium selections of California wines, plus domestic and imported beers.

There are five separate restaurants at the inn and country club, each featuring a distinct atmosphere. It was originally suggested that "Gentlemen not desiring to dine in evening dress may use the East dining room." Today, the inn's requirements of guests are not so stringent, but its self-imposed requirements for good food have not been relaxed.

An appetizing way to begin your meal is with the marinated herring. My personal choice would be to follow with the fillet of sole poached in champagne, but I'm told that the established winner is a generous cut of prime rib, with the Veal Oscar as a close runner-up.

After dining, it's entertaining to read the inscriptions etched into the huge fireplaces at either end of the lobby. Each is large enough to burn twelve-foot logs. Chiseled into the stones are the thoughts of Emerson, Thoreau, and Jefferson, and a few quotes that strain one's Latin to translate. But the philosophical inscription that seemed best suited to the era of the Grove Park Inn was "Be not simply good, be good for something!"

Grove Park Inn and Country Club is located on Macon Street in Asheville. Breakfast is served from 7:30 to 10:00 a.m., lunch from noon to 3:00 p.m., and dinner from 6:30 to 9:00 p.m., every day from April 21 to November 1. For reservations call (704) 252–2711.

GROVE PARK INN'S
STUFFED PORK TENDERLOIN

1 pork tenderloin, cleaned and excess fat removed	salt and pepper
6 dried apricots	3 slices bacon
6 dried prunes	2 to 3 tablespoons vegetable oil
1 apple	2 to 3 tablespoons heavy cream
¼ cup Calvados or brandy	

Soak apricots and prunes overnight in water. Peel apple and cut into 7 or 8 slices; marinate in Calvados.

Make a pocket in the tenderloin from head to tail. Put apples, apricots, and prunes inside. Close, season with salt and pepper, wrap in bacon, and sauté quickly in hot oil. Roast about 20 minutes in moderate oven, then flambé with Calvados. Remove tenderloin from oven and keep warm.

Add cream to the juices in the pan, and reduce a little, stirring constantly over medium heat. Season to taste.

Slice tenderloin, pour some sauce over it. Serve remaining sauce separately. Serves 3.

GROVE PARK INN'S
FRIED SWISS CHEESE IN BEER BATTER

1 cup flour
1 egg yolk
pinch of salt
1 ounce beer

2 egg whites
3 3-ounce slices
   Swiss cheese
oil for frying

Bring cheese to room temperature. Mix ½ cup flour, egg yolk, salt, and beer. Beat egg whites to stiff peaks and fold slowly into batter. Coat cheese slices with flour and dip in batter. Deep fry in vegetable oil. Serve with a salad. Serves 3.

GROVE PARK INN'S
FILLET OF SOLE IN CHAMPAGNE SAUCE

2 1-pound sole, filleted
   (can use flounder)
½ cup dry white wine
1 cup dry champagne
salt and pepper
1 bay leaf

dash of Worcestershire
   sauce
1 carrot, sliced
½ medium onion, sliced
½ cup heavy cream

Poach sole in white wine, ½ cup champagne, salt, pepper, bay leaf, Worcestershire sauce, carrot, and onions. When fillets are tender, remove from liquid and keep warm. Strain liquid, add rest of champagne and heavy cream. Reduce to a creamy consistency, stirring constantly over medium heat. Season to taste. Arrange fillets on a plate; cover with sauce.

Serve with parsley potatoes, if desired. Serves 2.

BILTMORE VILLAGE INNE
Asheville

BILTMORE VILLAGE
INNE

I hadn't realized that the pineapple is a symbol of welcome until I visited The Pineapple Room at the Biltmore Village Inne.

This quaint inn was once the home of one of the artisans who built Biltmore House. During the five years it took to construct Biltmore, the workers were housed in this special village, which had its own railroad for the purpose of transporting the building materials for the mansion. Other houses in the village are now interesting shops.

The house is reminiscent of an English cottage and its proprietors, the Files, are English; but the Inne has been patterned after a Williamsburg tavern, right down to its food. The thoroughly researched recipes make you feel as though you are tasting a part of America's past, which indeed you are if you order the Chicken Jefferson. It is recorded in White House records as Thomas Jefferson's favorite.

In discussing the recipes with Mrs. File, I was amused to find how many of them use alcohol; but a historian has stated that "Colonial drinking was an elaborate affair, as opulent and abundant as the food, and quite as necessary." If you do not consider it "necessary," then you can imbibe one of the imported teas at the restaurant's mid-afternoon high tea. It is served in the warmer months on a canopied deck overlooking an herb garden. If you've never had high tea, my advice is to try it with scones, cucumber sandwiches, fresh berries, and an assortment of tea cookies.

For a low-calorie meal, Mrs. File suggests the Florentine crepe or her lemon or strawberry soup. On weekends you are in for a special regalement of strolling musicians who sing old ballads as they play lute, recorder, and on occasion, harpsicord. Probably the most festive scene that the Inne has provoked was during a stopover for 800 railway travelers who had come to Asheville to enjoy the color of the fall leaves. The color took quite a different tone when the travelers heard the sound of the Inne's guardsman, who was dressed in Prince Charles Stuart costume, playing the bagpipe. Like a true piper, he drew the entire group to the Inne, where an impromptu street party was held on the spot.

Biltmore Village Inne is located at 5 Boston Way, Biltmore Village in Asheville. Lunch is served from 11:00 a. m. to 2:30 p. m., high tea from 2:30 to 5:00 p. m., and dinner from 6:00 to 9:30 p. m. For reservations call (704) 274–4100.

BILTMORE VILLAGE INNE'S
BRANDIED CRANBERRIES

1 package fresh cranberries	**2 to 3 tablespoons real**
½ cup or more dark brown	**butter**
sugar	**½ cup brandy**

Wash and stem cranberries. Place in 13- by 9- by 2-inch ovenproof pan. Dot with butter and sprinkle with brown sugar. Use more butter and sugar if needed. Pour ¼ cup brandy over top of cranberry mixture. Bake at 350 degrees for about 15 minutes, until bubbles begin to form on top. Stir with slotted spoon and add remaining brandy.

Can be flambéed and served at once. Serves 6 to 8.

BILTMORE VILLAGE INNE'S
CHICKEN JEFFERSON

4 large chicken breasts,	**2 cups whipping cream**
deboned	**salt and pepper**
1 stick butter	**nutmeg**
flour	**cayenne**
1 cup chicken stock	**¼ cup brandy**
(see Index)	

Cut chicken into finger-sized pieces. Salt and let stand a few minutes. Heat half of butter in a heavy skillet until it bubbles. Dredge meat with flour, and brown lightly; place meat in baking dish. Place remaining butter into skillet. Scrape skillet and add three tablespoons flour, whisking rapidly to make a roux. Gradually add the chicken stock, continuing to whisk the sauce until smooth and bubbly. Add the cream and seasonings. Sauce should be the consistency of very heavy cream; if it is too thick, add a little milk. Add the brandy and stir. Pour sauce over chicken. Cover and cook at 350 degrees for 15 minutes, or until chicken is tender. Serve immediately. Serves 4 to 6.

BILTMORE VILLAGE INNE'S
PEA PUDDING

1 pound dried green peas	salt
2 strips bacon	white pepper
1 small carrot	rosemary
2 stalks celery	pinch of sugar
1 medium onion	2 tablespoons butter
2 cloves garlic, crushed	½ cup sour cream
1 teaspoon nutmeg	parsley or mint

Put peas in large, deep bowl; cover with cold water and let soak overnight.

Strain; put in a large, heavy pot; and cover with fresh, cold water. Add bacon, and bring slowly to a boil. Cook until barely tender. Chop carrots, celery, and onion, and add with seasonings. Simmer slowly until peas are very soft and have absorbed most of the water. Stir frequently. Place mixture in blender, adding butter and sour cream. Blend to puree consistency. Pour in flat serving dish and garnish with parsley or mint. Serves 6 to 8.

DEERPARK
Asheville

DEERPARK

Name one other restaurant in North Carolina where, as you dine, you can watch a herd of seventy-five deer prance before your eyes. I can think only of Deerpark Restaurant, located on the Biltmore Estate. You have access to this privilege because in the 1880's George Vanderbilt instructed his landscape designer, Frederick Law Olmstead, to set aside this area as a deer preserve.

Deerpark is approached by a winding three-mile drive through a natural forest with pools, springs, and streams. The rolling landscape, which leans so subtly against the Smoky Mountains and hides the castlelike Biltmore House, gives the illusion of a fairy tale. Deerpark's building, which has such English touches as a half-timbered and pebble-dash facade, was originally Biltmore's dairy barn. Vanderbilt's interest in self-sufficiency and the proper use of land is responsible for the dairy products that continue to be produced from the Biltmore Dairy, and which you can enjoy when you visit Deerpark. If you are lucky, you may also sip one of the premium wines that are being made on the Biltmore Estate. I say "lucky" because the five-year-old wine operation has not, at this writing, been able to produce wines as quickly as they can be sold.

The day I lunched alfresco in the restaurant's flower-filled garden courtyard, the wine supply was almost depleted. By the time you read this passage, however, a new crop will have completed its fermentation process and you may have a better chance of securing a glass of wine with your lunch. The white wine is excellent with my favorite entrée, the Deerpark Seafood Salad. This is a tastefully inventive arrangement of boiled shrimp and crab legs circled with avocado slices. If you bypass the avocadoes, it is a perfect low-calorie meal. My luncheon companion allowed me to taste-test his chopped sirloin. What a surprise! The grilled meat was topped with a slice of Swiss cheese, fried onions and fresh mushrooms, and a Burgundy sauce. That savory concoction was set off by a unique baked apple.

The restaurant's cooks let me in on the secret of their new dessert. The apple-nut ice cream is made with honey, and it can't realistically be reproduced in your kitchen, so try it while you're there. I was planning just to taste the carrot and German chocolate cakes, but I devoured all of the carrot and half of the chocolate! So much for the calories my salad saved, but it was worth it.

Do set aside enough time to tour the majestic Biltmore House and Gardens.

Deerpark is located on the Biltmore Estate, which is off U. S. 25 at Asheville. Lunch is served from 11:00 a. m. to 3:00 p. m. daily, from March 15 to December. Deerpark serves dinner only to large private parties. For reservations call (704) 274–1776.

DEERPARK'S CHICKEN TERIYAKI

4 chicken breasts, deboned	1 pint cherry tomatoes
4 tablespoons butter	2 medium-sized peppers,
½ cup Chablis	cut in thin strips
1 4-ounce can bamboo	¼ cup soy sauce
shoots	1 teaspoon sugar

Melt butter in skillet and add deboned chicken; cover and braise chicken on both sides. Remove chicken. Sauté vegetables, then stir in wine, soy sauce, and sugar. Add chicken and cook at much lower heat for about 10 minutes, until chicken absorbs flavor.

Serve with long-grain wild rice. Serves 6.

DEERPARK'S BAKED APPLES

6 to 8 apples, winesap	1 cup sliced almonds
or rome	pinch of nutmeg
honey	pinch of cinnamon
½ cup raisins	

Halve and core apples. Mix honey, raisins, almonds, nutmeg, and cinnamon. Fill each apple half with mixture and place in a greased flat baking dish. Bake at 350 degrees for 12 to 15 minutes. Serves 10 to 12.

DEERPARK'S GLAZED CARROTS

6 to 8 carrots
1 6-ounce can concentrated
  orange juice

½ cup sauterne
pinch of salt

Shred carrots and set aside. Mix sauterne, orange juice concentrate, and salt in a saucepan; add carrots and simmer until tender, an hour or more. Serves 8.

DEERPARK'S VEAL A LA CARDINALE

3 veal cutlets
2 eggs
bread crumbs
4 tablespoons oil
4 tablespoons butter

3 slices Prosciutto ham
3 slices mozzarella cheese
2 cups sliced mushrooms
1 teaspoon chopped fresh
  basil or parsley

Pound veal to less than ¼ inch thick. Dip veal into beaten eggs, then into bread crumbs. Sauté in butter until golden brown on each side. Remove to baking dish. On each piece of veal, place 1 slice ham and 1 slice cheese. Bake at 400 degrees until cheese melts. Meanwhile, in same frying pan used for veal, sauté mushrooms with herbs. Put mushrooms over veal.

Serve with wild rice. Serves 3.

THE MARKET PLACE
Asheville

THE MARKET PLACE The most interesting historical tidbit about the building from the early twenties that now houses The Market Place restaurant is that it was once a printing shop whose owners fired Walt Disney. Speculations concerning his termination are limited only by your imagination, but the favored explanation is that printers use artists primarily for printing, not cartooning.

I am happy to report, however, that the owners and renovators of The Market Place were not handicapped by the shortsightedness of the previous owners. Their conversion has given the restaurant a sophisticated tropical decor that blends successfully with its classic continental cuisine. The most attractive feature of this unusual decor is the wainscoting made of terra-cotta tiles surrounded by an Art Nouveau metalwork that once decorated railroad dining cars. I really loved the comfortable bamboo chairs, which are smartly cushioned in muted tropical prints. Circle down the stairs and you are greeted by an entirely different but equally pleasant atmosphere in The Grill Room.

Upstairs amidst the bamboo, I was made to feel, as the restaurant's motto suggests, that The Market Place was responsible for my well-being as long as I was under its roof. When I explained to the chef and co-owner, Mark Rosenstein, that I had been overindulging lately, he suggested the poached trout and said I couldn't have anything lighter without eating air. He was right, and my palate was not underprivileged with this choice. For a different dining taste you might try the grilled lamb or Chicken St. James.

The underground wine cellar is kept at sixty-two degrees. In the amended words of the poet Henry Aldrich, The Market Place suggests, "If all be true I do think, there are three reasons we should drink: Good wine—a friend—or being dry." On that, and the too-delicious-to-describe multi-layer Marjolaine Cake, I will bid you a sumptuous dining experience at The Market Place.

The Market Place is located at 10 North Market Street in Asheville. Dinner is served from 6:00 to 10:00 p. m. Monday through Saturday. For reservations call (704) 252–4162.

THE MARKET PLACE'S MARJOLAINE CAKE

Almond praline:
1 cup sugar   **½ cup almonds, toasted**

Vanilla cream:
2 cups whipping cream   **1 teaspoon vanilla**
4 tablespoons sugar

Chocolate cream:
1½ cups semi-sweet   **1¼ cups sour cream**
** chocolate**

Meringues:
⅝ cup almonds, toasted   **¼ cup plain flour**
⅞ cup filberts, toasted   **9 egg whites**
¼ cup sugar

To make almond praline, caramelize 1 cup sugar. Pour into pan; cool and grind with ½ cup almonds. Cover and set aside.

To make vanilla cream, whip cream with sugar and vanilla until thick peaks form. Place in a strainer and let sit overnight at 65 degrees.

To make meringues, grind together filberts and almonds; add ¼ cup each sugar and flour. Whip egg whites until stiff and fold nut mixture carefully into them, blending thoroughly. Line two 12- by 18-inch baking sheets with silicone baking paper. Draw two rectangles 4 by 16 inches on each piece of paper. Divide mixture into four equal parts on the sheets and spread with a spatula to fill rectangles. Meringue should be ½ inch thick. Bake at 300 degrees for 1¼ to 1¾ hours, or until slightly crispy. Cool and preserve.

On the next day, combine chocolate and sour cream in a double boiler and heat until chocolate melts; keep warm. Mix ½ cup almond praline into ½ chocolate mixture.

To assemble cake, place a layer of meringue on a serving dish. Spread evenly with all of chocolate and praline mixture. Top with second meringue and spread that with ⅓ of chocolate and sour cream mixture. Refrigerate 10 minutes, then place third meringue on top and spread all of vanilla cream. Refrigerate 10 to 15 minutes, then top with last meringue and cover cake completely with remaining chocolate and sour cream mixture. Refrigerate for 12 to 24 hours before serving. Serves 16 to 20.

THE MARKET PLACE'S
GRILLED LAMB WITH MUSTARD

1 leg of lamb, deboned,
  butterflied, and cut
  into ½-inch steaks
2 tablespoons olive oil
2 tablespoons chopped
  fresh oregano

salt and pepper
cognac
4 tablespoons Dijon
  mustard
Béarnaise sauce
  (see Index)

With a brush, coat lamb steaks with olive oil. Place on grill. Sprinkle with half the oregano, salt, and pepper. Cook 6 to 8 minutes, until blood shows. Turn and sprinkle other side with oregano, salt, and pepper. Cook 4 to 8 minutes, depending on degree of doneness desired.

Sprinkle cognac over top and ignite. Spread mustard on top and serve with Béarnaise sauce. Serves 8.

JARRETT HOUSE
Dillsboro

JARRETT HOUSE The first words I overheard upon entering the dining room of Jarrett House were, "I could make a whole meal out of these biscuits alone." Sampling one of the biscuits before my fresh rainbow trout arrived, I agreed with the biscuit lover, but then I didn't do too badly with the candied apples, green beans, beets, potatoes, cole-slaw, and iced tea sweetened with honey. All around me I heard acclamations for the peach cobbler, but Jim Hartbarger, the inn's owner and a former college basketball coach, said I should try the vinegar pie. I must admit the name puts you off, but I assure you the taste will not. It was, as his wife Jean described it, like a pecan pie without the pecans. Don't think that decalorizes it; there's no such thing as a low-calorie meal at Jarrett House.

Although I would definitely again order the trout, which is fresh from a neighboring hatchery, you might prefer the country ham or fried chicken in "all you can stuff" quantities.

The 1886 house will bring back childhood memories of stuffing yourself at grandma's. It has been "prettied up" a bit by the Hartbargers, but they have been careful not to disturb its quaint atmosphere. The Victorian-style parlor still looks as if my grandmother should be rocking beneath the lace wall hanging with the Twenty-third Psalm on it. The three-story rambling white structure, built by the man for whom Dills-boro was named, is encircled with wrought iron porches. The turn-of-the-century traveler could get a bed and feed for his horse for twenty-five cents. Meals were a dime extra. Later the inn was sold to Jarrett, who cured hams upstairs and in the basement near the natural sulphur spring pro-duced a concoction that neighbors said smelled peculiarly like alcohol. That was not the only scandal to come out of the house. During the roar of the twenties two young ladies from Edenton are reported to have shocked half the town when they lit up cigarettes right on the front porch.

The inn is in a dry county, but brown bagging is permitted. The guests partake of refreshment in the upstairs lounge, but for some reason never feel comfortable bringing their brown bags downstairs to the dining room.

You'll enjoy the food, and if you have the opportunity to sleep in one of the bedrooms furnished with antiques and lacking the cumbersome paraphernalia of telephones and television, then you'll relax right into the spirit, especially with the mountains nestling right behind the inn's back door.

The Jarrett House is located at the intersection of U. S. 19A–23 and U. S. 441–19A in Dillsboro. Breakfast is served from 7:00 to 10:30 a. m., lunch from 11:30 a. m. to 2:00 p. m., and dinner from 5:00 to 8:30 p. m., daily from April through October. For reservations call (704) 586–9164.

JARRETT HOUSE'S PICKLED BEETS

1 onion	**½ cup vinegar**
1 can beets	**1 cup sugar**

Slice onion thin. Mix in a bowl with beets, juice, vinegar, and sugar. Cover and refrigerate for several hours or overnight. Serves 4 to 6.

JARRETT HOUSE'S SQUASH CASSEROLE

1 pound fresh squash, or canned	**5 or 6 leftover biscuits crumbled fine, or corn bread**
1 medium onion, chopped	**salt and pepper**
6 slices bacon, cooked and crumbled	**3 to 4 tablespoons melted butter**

Cook squash until almost tender. Drain and place in greased flat, ovenproof pan. Add onions, bacon, and crumbled biscuits on top. Pour melted butter over biscuits. Bake at 350 degrees for 30 minutes, or until golden brown. Serves 4.

JARRETT HOUSE'S VINEGAR PIE

1 stick margarine, melted
2 tablespoons flour
2 tablespoons vinegar
1½ cups sugar

1 tablespoon vanilla
  extract
3 eggs
1 9-inch pie shell, unbaked

Combine first six ingredients, blending well. Pour into pie shell. Bake at 300 degrees for 45 minutes.

HIGH HAMPTON INN
Cashiers

HIGH HAMPTON INN After sitting for a bit on the back porch balcony at High Hampton Inn, a feeling of serenity begins to permeate your being. Initially, however, the view of Hampton Lake curled at the base of Rock and Chimney Top mountains elicits an emotion no less than exhilaration.

Spectacles always make me hungry, so when I went through the luncheon buffet I helped myself to generous portions of Spanish Eggplant, corned beef and cabbage, corn relish, macaroni salad, a green salad, several sausage bread muffins, and lemonade.

There are so many activities at this family-style inn—including horseback riding, tennis, golf, swimming, skeet shooting, fishing, and canoeing—that there is ample opportunity to burn calories. But if rocking on the porch is your definition of exercise, as it often is mine, then take advantage of the salads and fresh melon selections for lunch and concentrate on broiled fish at the dinner buffet. I must point out, however, that you would miss the inn's special dessert, Black Bottom Pie, which would be a true deprivation.

The present structure at High Hampton was built in 1922 by E. L. McKee, the grandfather of the present owner. However, the socializing there dates back to 1791, when Wade Hampton, the Confederate general and South Carolina governor, built his retreat in the Cashiers valley. He was not the only prominent figure to own the property; his daughter Caroline married Dr. William Steward Halstead, who was head of Johns Hopkins Hospital and is credited with inventing the rubber surgical gloves, localized anesthesia, and a surgical technique that is still practiced in some hospitals.

Caroline much preferred the unpretentious life of supervising the landscaping of her dahlia garden at High Hampton to the society life of Baltimore. Dahlias continue to be nurtured at the inn, and they provide a cheerful addition to the bucolic surroundings.

High Hampton Inn and Country Club is located on N. C. 107, two miles south of Cashiers. It is open daily from April 1 to November 1, and on Thanksgiving weekend. Breakfast is served from 8:00 to 9:30 a.m.; lunch from 12:30 to 2:15 p.m.; and dinner from 6:30 to 8:00 p. m. The Rocky Mountain Lounge opens at 4:00 p. m. For reservations call (704) 743-2411.

HIGH HAMPTON INN'S SPANISH EGGPLANT

1 large eggplant
1 teaspoon salt
4 tablespoons butter
½ cup chopped onions
½ cup chopped green
   peppers
1 14½-ounce can tomatoes
¼ cup brown sugar

4 tablespoons Parmesan
   cheese
1 teaspoon salt, or to taste
½ teaspoon or more white
   pepper
½ teaspoon garlic powder
   or salt
½ cup bread crumbs

In a saucepan dissolve 1 teaspoon salt in a pint of water. Peel and cube eggplant and parboil in salted water. In separate skillet melt 2 tablespoons butter and sauté onions and peppers; set aside. Drain eggplant and tomatoes and mix together in greased casserole. Season with brown sugar, 2 tablespoons Parmesan cheese, salt, pepper, and garlic. Add onions and peppers and mix thoroughly. Melt remaining butter and drizzle over bread crumbs. Sprinkle crumbs and remaining cheese over vegetables. Bake at 350 degrees for 35 to 40 minutes or until brown. Serves 4.

HIGH HAMPTON INN'S BLACK BOTTOM PIE

Crust:
1 ½ cups crushed Zwieback
¼ cup powdered sugar

6 tablespoons melted butter
1 teaspoon cinnamon

Chocolate filling:
1 tablespoon gelatin

¼ cup cold water

2 cups half and half
4 egg yolks (reserve whites)
1 cup sugar
4 teaspoons cornstarch

½ teaspoon vanilla
1½ ounces chocolate,
  melted

To complete custard filling:
3 egg whites
¼ teaspoon salt
¼ teaspoon cream of tartar

¼ cup sugar
1 teaspoon almond extract

Topping:
1 cup heavy whipping
  cream

2 tablespoons powdered
  sugar

For crust, mix all ingredients well and pat out evenly into a deep 9-inch pie pan. Bake at 300 degrees for 15 minutes. Cool.

For chocolate filling, soak gelatin in cold water. Scald half and half. Beat egg yolks, and add sugar and cornstarch. Place in double boiler and stir half and half in gradually; keep stirring until custard coats a spoon, about 20 minutes. Remove from heat and pour out 1 cup of custard. Add chocolate to cup of custard and beat until well blended and cool. Add vanilla and pour into pie shell. Add gelatin to remaining custard; cool, but do not allow to stiffen.

To complete custard filling, make stiff meringue by beating egg whites with salt until frothy. Add cream of tartar and beat until stiff enough to hold a peak, then gradually beat in sugar until very stiff. While remaining custard is still soft, fold in meringue very gently, blend in almond extract, and chill. Pour over chocolate custard.

For the topping, whip the cream, add powdered sugar, and spread over top of pie. Chill until served.

RANDOLPH HOUSE
Bryson City

RANDOLPH HOUSE As your old oak rocker shuttles back and forth on the front porch of Randolph House, the flicker of the evening's fireflies is accompanied by the sound of crickets. This place was once called Peaceful Lodge, and with good reason.

No one races to keep up with schedules here. There are no clocks, radios, or televisions; changes in time are marked by the varyirtg aromas issuing from Ruth Adams' kitchen. The morning is signaled by the scent of bacon and coffee (which will accompany eggs, grits, sweet rolls, and jam that was made in the summer kitchen). Dinner is announced by the summoning smell of angel biscuits.

That heavenly fragrance led my daughter Heather and me from our rocking chairs on the porch and into the antique-filled dining room of Randolph House. The residents of Bryson City called this "the mansion on the hill" when the house was constructed in 1895. The house was built by lumber tycoon Amos Frye and his wife Lillian, the town's first practicing female attorney. Being an enterprising couple, the Fryes used their mansion not only to entertain their guests, but also as a lodge and a gift shop.

As was the custom of the day, Mrs. Frye's unmarried sister, Eugenia Rowe, lived with the family. She was an accomplished artist schooled in the Flemish tradition. In the lobby of the inn is Eugenia's rendition of Adam and Eve fleeing the Garden of Eden. Because Eve's filmy dress is inching "indecently" up her thigh, Eugenia became known about town as an eccentric. Consequently, she spent many of her years alone in the attic, painting her visions. In a painting that hung across from me at dinner, grapes glistened so deliciously that I wanted to pick them.

Instead, I drank my dry white wine, a Wente Pinot Chardonnay, which was a perfect accompaniment for my delicious Veal Scallopini. Obviously, Mrs. Adams' food is not strictly Southern. Even though Heather ate every bite of her very Southern fried chicken, the cuisine is heavily influenced by gourmet fare of other parts of the world. The wonderful poppy seed torte with raspberry sauce is an excellent case in point. This dish is not exactly a calorie cutter, but Mrs. Adams is happy to prepare something to suit your diet if she is given adequate advance notice.

Randolph House is located in Bryson City on Fryemont Road. From Asheville follow I-40 west to U.S. 19A-23, and take the second Bryson City exit. Breakfast is served from 8:00 to 9:30 a.m., and dinner from 6:00 to 8:30 p.m., daily from April through October. For reservations call (704) 488-3472.

RANDOLPH HOUSE'S ANGEL BISCUITS

1½ packages dry yeast
3 tablespoons warm water
5 cups self-rising flour
¼ cup sugar
¼ teaspoon salt
1½ cups shortening
2½ cups buttermilk

Combine yeast and warm water; let stand five minutes. Combine dry ingredients in large bowl; cut in shortening until mixture resembles coarse crumbs. Add buttermilk to yeast mixture and mix with dry ingredients. Beat vigorously. Cover; let rise for two hours.

Beat dough again. Cut and fill greased muffin tins half full, and let rise to double size. Bake at 450 degrees for 7 to 10 minutes. Yields about 60 biscuits. Dough will keep in refrigerator for about a week.

RANDOLPH HOUSE'S POPPY SEED TORTE

Pastry:
⅓ cup poppy seeds
¾ cup milk
¾ cup butter
1½ cups sugar
1½ teaspoons vanilla
2 cups cake four, sifted
2½ teaspoons baking powder
¼ teaspoon salt
4 egg whites, stiffly beaten

199

Filling:

½ cup sugar

1 tablespoon cornstarch

1½ cups milk

4 egg yolks, slightly beaten

1 teaspoon vanilla

¼ cup chopped walnuts

For pastry, soak seeds in milk for one hour. Cream butter and sugar in electric mixer until fluffy. Mix in vanilla, milk, and seeds. Sift together remaining dry ingredients and stir into creamed mixture. Fold in egg whites. Bake in four well-greased and lightly floured round cake pans, making very thin layers. Bake at 375 degrees for 15 to 20 minutes. Cool and remove from pans.

For filling, mix sugar and cornstarch. Combine milk and egg yolks, and stir gradually into sugar mixture. Cook, stirring, until bubbly. Cool. Add vanilla and walnuts to mixture. Spread filling between layers of pastry. Chill two to three hours, then sift confectioners' sugar on top. Serve with raspberry sauce (see recipe below).

RANDOLPH HOUSE'S RASPBERRY SAUCE

1 package frozen
  raspberries

¾ cup sugar

1 tablespoon cornstarch

1 tablespoon butter

Combine all ingredients in a saucepan and cook over medium heat until slightly thickened. Chill and serve over poppy seed torte with cream.

INDEX

Ice Creams and Sherbets:
Banana Ice Cream, Spoon's 128
Espresso Ice Cream, La
  Résidence 72
Grapefruit Sorbet, Glendale
  Springs 156
Kiss, Island Inn 8
Raspberry Grand Marnier,
  Angus Barn 52
Strawberry Cheesecake Ice
  Cream, Spoon's 128

Miscellaneous:
Apple Strudel, Jolly Mill 144
Chocolate Mousse, French
  Country Inn 48
Crepes Fitzgerald, Villa Téo 64
Lemon Soufflé, Salem Cotton
  Co. 103
Noodle Pudding, Salem Cotton
  Co. 104
Poppy Seed Torte, Randolph
  House 199
Raspberry Sauce, Randolph
  House 200
Raspberry Soufflé, Eli's 132
Strawberry Crepes, Clawson's
  16
Tartufi, Lamp Lighter 124

Pies:
Aunt Betty's Coconut Pie,
  Poplar Grove 28
Bakewell Tart, Nickleby's 135
Black Bottom Pie, High
  Hampton Inn 195
Bourbon Pecan Pie,
  Fearrington House 68
Chocolate Chess Pie, Angus
  Barn 52

Mud Pie, Country Inn 132
Oatmeal Pie, Weaverville
  Milling Co. 172
Peach and Blueberry Cobbler,
  Weaverville Milling Co. 171
Peanut Butter Pie, Eli's 112
Pie Pastry, Fearrington House
  68
Rhubarb Cobbler, Shatley
  Springs 148
Sour Cream Pie, Nu-Wray Inn
  167
Tar Heel Pie, Tanglewood
  Manor House 108
Vinegar Pie, Jarrett House 192

ENTREES
Egg Dishes:
Asparagus Omelet, Glendale
  Springs 156
Quiche Lorraine, Graham
  House 39

Fowl:
Chicken Cordon Bleu, Zevely
  House 96
Chicken Crepes, Graham
  House 40
Chicken Elaine, Island Inn 7
Chicken Fantastic, Poplar
  Grove 28
Chicken Jefferson, Biltmore
  Village Inne 179
Chicken, Oven-Crisp, Country
  Inn 139
Chicken Pecan, Lamp Lighter
  123
Chicken Regina, O'Neill's 120
Chicken, Sour Cream,
  Stemmerman's 32

Chicken Suprémes Pommery, Sudi's 56
Chicken Teriyaki, Deerpark 183
Chicken with Basil Sauce, La Chaudière 100
Coq au Vin, Green Park Inn 163
Country Captain, Harvey Mansion 19
Duck Stroganoff, Salem Cotton Co. 103
Quail Pie, Country Squire 44

Meat:
Filet Mignon with Sauce Raifort, La Résidence 71
Ham in Rye Dough, Manor Inn 75
Ham in White Wine Sauce, French Country Inn 47
Lamb, Grilled with Mustard, Market Place 188
Original Dirigible, Clawson's 16
Pork Chops, Stuffed, Green Park Inn 164
Pork Loin, Roast, Fearrington House 67
Pork Tenderloin, Grove Park Inn 175
Pork with Mustard Sauce, La Résidence 72
Steak and Oyster Pie, Nickleby's 136
Steak, Kailua, Country Squire 43
Steak, Pepper, River Forest Manor 4
Stew, Irish, O'Neill's 119

Sub on a Spud, Spoon's 127
Veal a la Cardinale, Deerpark 184
Veal in the Trees, Elms 83
Veal Oscar, Zevely House 95
Veal Sweetbreads in Madeira Sauce, Riverview 36
Wiener Schnitzel Holstein, Salem Tavern 91

Seafood:
Crab Cakes, Country Inn 140
Crab Cakes Supreme, Villa Téo 64
Crab Casserole, Pamlico, River Forest Manor 4
Crab, Deviled, Clawson's 15
Fish Stew, Nickleby's 136
Flounder Marguery, Stemmerman's 31
Oyster Pie, Steak and, Nickleby's 136
Oysters Riverview 35
Seafood Salad, Green Park Inn 163
Shrimp and Chicken Ariosto, Island Inn 8
Shrimp, Broiled Barbecued, Country Inn 139
Shrimp, Calabash, Kathryn's 116
Shrimp in Caper Butter, Pelican Inn 12
Shrimp Port Gibson, Marinated, Tanglewood Manor House 107
Shrimp Scampi, Riverview 35
Shrimp Special, Jolly Mill 143
Shrimp Victoria, Depot 87

Library of Congress Cataloging in Publication Data

O'Brien, Dawn.
  North Carolina's historic restaurants and their
recipes.

  Includes index.
  1. Cookery, American—North Carolina. 2. Restaurants,
lunch rooms, etc.—North Carolina. 3. Historic buildings
—North Carolina. I. Title.
TX715.0'285 1983b   641.5'09756   83-21557
ISBN 0-89587-034-7